AF207629

INVESTIGATING

AN INQUIRY EARTH SCIENCE PROGRAM

INVESTIGATING OCEANS

Michael J. Smith Ph.D.
American Geological Institute

John B. Southard Ph.D.
Massachussetts Institute of Technology

Colin Mably
Curriculum Developer

Developed by the American Geological Institute
Supported by the National Science Foundation and
the American Geological Institute Foundation

Published by
It's About Time Inc., Armonk, NY

It's About Time, Inc.

84 Business Park Drive, Armonk, NY 10504
Phone (914) 273-2233 Fax (914) 273-2227
Toll Free (888) 698-TIME
www.Its-About-Time.com

Publisher
Laurie Kreindler

Project Editor Ruta Demery	**Creative Artwork** Dennis Falcon	**Senior Photo Consultant** Bruce F. Molnia
Design John Nordland	**Safety Reviewer** Edward Robeck	**Photo Research** Caitlin Callahan Eric Shih
Studio Manager Joan Lee	**Production** Burmar Technical Corporation	**Contributing Writer** William Jones
Associate Editor Al Mari	**Technical Art** Armstrong/Burmar	

Illustrations and Photos
O9, Adobe Image Library
O21, O42, O43, technical art by Stuart Armstrong
Oxi (bottom left), O39, P. Auster, NOAA
O4, O12, O15, O16, O32, O38, O45, O50, O51, O52, O57, illustrations by Burmar Technical Corporation
O20, O26, O33, Armstrong/Burmar
O6, Cargill Salt Asia Pacific
O10 (A), O36, O53 (top right, bottom left, bottom right), O55, Digital Stock Corporation
O53 (top right), Harry Dowsett, USGS
Ov, Oxii, O3, O11, O12, O23, O30, O40, O48, O58, O61, illustrations by Dennis Falcon
O44, R.W. Grigg, University of Hawaii
O19, Bruce F. Molnia
O35, NOAA
Oxi (top photos, bottom right), Oxii, O1, O7, O10 (B, C, D), O17, O27, O47, O56 (top), O59, PhotoDisc
O29, left, Frank Ruopoli, NOAA Coastal Services Center
O25, Walter Smith, NASA; David Sandwell, Scripps Institution of Oceanography
O56 (bottom), United States Geological Survey, Biology

All student activities in this textbook have been designed to be as safe as possible, and have been reviewed by professionals specifically for that purpose. As well, appropriate warnings concerning potential safety hazards are included where applicable to particular activities. However, responsibility for safety remains with the student, the classroom teacher, the school principals, and the school board.

Investigating Earth Systems™ is a registered trademark of the American Geological Institute. Registered names and trademarks, etc. used in this publication, even without specific indication thereof, are not to be considered unprotected by law.

It's About Time™ is a registered trademark of It's About Time, Inc. Registered names and trademarks, etc. used in this publication, even without specific indication thereof, are not to be considered unprotected by law.

Care has been taken to trace the ownership of copyright material contained in this publication. The publisher will gladly receive any information that will rectify any reference or credit line in subsequent editions.

Printed and bound in the United States of America

ISBN #1-58591-074-0

1 2 3 4 5 QC 05 04 03 02 01

This project was supported, in part, by the
National Science Foundation (grant no. 9353035)

Opinions expressed are those of the authors and not necessarily those of the National Science Foundation or the donors of the American Geological Institute Foundation.

Acknowledgements

Principal Investigator

Michael Smith is Director of Education at the American Geological Institute in Alexandria, Virginia. Dr. Smith worked as an exploration geologist and hydrogeologist. He began his Earth science teaching career with Shady Side Academy in Pittsburgh, PA in 1988 and most recently taught Earth Science at the Charter School of Wilmington, DE. He earned a doctorate from the University of Pittsburgh's Cognitive Studies in Education Program and joined the faculty of the University of Delaware School of Education in 1995. Dr. Smith received the Outstanding Earth Science Teacher Award for Pennsylvania from the National Association of Geoscience Teachers in 1991, served as Secretary of the National Earth Science Teachers Association, and is a reviewer for Science Education and The Journal of Research in Science Teaching. He worked on the Delaware Teacher Standards, Delaware Science Assessment, National Board of Teacher Certification, and AAAS Project 2061 Curriculum Evaluation programs.

Senior Writer

John Southard received his undergraduate degree from the Massachusetts Institute of Technology in 1960 and his doctorate in geology from Harvard University in 1966. After a National Science Foundation postdoctoral fellowship at the California Institute of Technology, he joined the faculty at the Massachusetts Institute of Technology, where he is currently Professor of Geology. He was awarded the MIT School of Science teaching prize in 1989 and was one of the first cohorts of first MacVicar Fellows at MIT, in recognition of excellence in undergraduate teaching. He has taught numerous undergraduate courses in introductory geology, sedimentary geology, field geology, and environmental Earth science both at MIT and in Harvard's adult education program. He was editor of the Journal of Sedimentary Petrology from 1992 to 1996, and he continues to do technical editing of scientific books and papers for SEPM, a professional society for sedimentary geology.

Project Director/Curriculum Designer

Colin Mably has been a key curriculum developer for several NSF-supported national curriculum projects. As learning materials designer to the American Geological Institute, he has directed the design and development of the IES curriculum modules and also training workshops for pilot and field-test teachers.

Project Team

Marcus Milling
Executive Director - AGI, VA

Michael Smith
Principal Investigator - Director
of Education - AGI, VA

Colin Mably
Project Director/Curriculum
Designer - Educational
Visions, MD

Fred Finley
Project Evaluator
University of Minnesota, MN

Lynn Lindow
Pilot Test Evaluator
University of Minnesota, MN

Harvey Rosenbaum
Field Test Evaluator
Montgomery School
District, MD

Ann Benbow
Project Advisor - American
Chemical Society, DC

Robert Ridky
Original Project Director
University of Maryland, MD

Chip Groat
Original Principal Investigator -
University of Texas
El Paso, TX

Marilyn Suiter
Original Co-principal
Investigator - AGI, VA

William Houston
Project Manager

Eric Shih - Project Assistant

Original and Contributing Authors

Oceans
George Dawson
Florida State University, FL

Joseph F. Donoghue
Florida State University, FL

Ann Benbow
American Chemical Society

Michael Smith
American Geological Institute

Soil
Robert Ridky
University of Maryland, MD

Colin Mably - LaPlata, MD

John Southard
Massachusetts Institute of
Technology, MA

Michael Smith
American Geological Institute

Fossils
Robert Gastaldo
Colby College, ME

Colin Mably - LaPlata, MD

Michael Smith
American Geological Institute

Climate and Weather
Mike Mogil
How the Weather Works, MD

Ann Benbow
American Chemical Society

Michael Smith
American Geological Institute

Energy Resources
Laurie Martin-Vermilyea
American Geological Institute

Michael Smith
American Geological Institute

Dynamic Planet
Michael Smith
American Geological Institute

Rocks and Landforms
Michael Smith
American Geological Institute

Water as a Resource
Ann Benbow
American Chemical Society

Michael Smith
American Geological Institute

Materials and Minerals
Mary Poulton
University of Arizona, AZ

Colin Mably - LaPlata, MD

Michael Smith
American Geological Institute

Advisory Board

Jane Crowder
Middle School Teacher, WA

Kerry Davidson
Louisiana Board of Regents, LA

Joseph D. Exline
Educational Consultant, VA

Louis A. Fernandez
California State University, CA

Frank Watt Ireton
National Earth Science Teachers
Association, DC

LeRoy Lee
Wisconsin Academy of Sciences,
Arts and Letters, WI

Donald W. Lewis
Chevron Corporation, CA

James V. O'Connor (deceased)
University of the District of
Columbia, DC

Roger A. Pielke Sr.
Colorado State University, CO

Dorothy Stout
Cypress College, CA

Lois Veath
Advisory Board Chairperson
Chadron State College, NE

Pilot Test Teachers

Debbie Bambino
Philadelphia, PA

Barbara Barden - Rittman, OH

Louisa Bliss - Bethlehem, NH

Mike Bradshaw - Houston TX

Greta Branch - Reno, NV

Garnetta Chain - Piscataway, NJ

Roy Chambers Portland, OR

Laurie Corbett - Sayre, PA

James Cole - New York, NY

Collette Craig - Reno, NV

Anne Douglas - Houston, TX

Jacqueline Dubin - Roslyn, PA

Jane Evans - Media, PA

Gail Gant - Houston, TX

Joan Gentry - Houston, TX

Pat Gram - Aurora, OH

Robert Haffner - Akron, OH

Joe Hampel - Swarthmore, PA

Wayne Hayes - West Green, GA

Mark Johnson - Reno, NV

Cheryl Joloza - Philadelphia, PA

Jeff Luckey - Houston, TX

Karen Luniewski
Reisterstown, MD

Cassie Major - Plainfield, VT

Carol Miller - Houston, TX

Melissa Murray - Reno, NV

Mary-Lou Northrop
North Kingstown, RI

Keith Olive - Ellensburg, WA

Tracey Oliver - Philadelphia, PA

Nicole Pfister - Londonderry, VT

Beth Price - Reno, NV

Joyce Ramig - Houston, TX

Julie Revilla - Woodbridge, VA

Steve Roberts - Meredith, NH

Cheryl Skipworth
Philadelphia, PA

Brent Stenson - Valdosta, GA

Elva Stout - Evans, GA

Regina Toscani
Philadelphia, PA

Bill Waterhouse
North Woodstock, NH

Leonard White
Philadelphia, PA

Paul Williams - Lowerford, VT

Bob Zafran - San Jose, CA

Missi Zender - Twinsburg, OH

Field Test Teachers

Eric Anderson - Carson City, NV

Katie Bauer - Rockport, ME

Kathleen Berdel - Philadelphia, PA

Wanda Blake - Macon, GA

Beverly Bowers
Mannington, WV

Rick Chiera - Monroe Falls, OH

Don Cole - Akron, OH

Patte Cotner - Bossier City, LA

Johnny DeFreese - Haughton, LA

Mary Devine - Astoria, NY

Cheryl Dodes - Queens, NY

Brenda Engstrom - Warwick, RI

Lisa Gioe-Cordi - Brooklyn, NY

Pat Gram - Aurora, OH

Mark Johnson - Reno, NV

Chicory Koren - Kent, OH

Marilyn Krupnick
Philadelphia, PA

Melissa Loftin - Bossier City, LA

Janet Lundy - Reno, NV

Vaughn Martin - Easton, ME

Anita Mathis - Fort Valley, GA

Laurie Newton - Truckee, NV

Debbie O'Gorman - Reno, NV

Joe Parlier - Barnesville, GA

Sunny Posey - Bossier City, LA

Beth Price - Reno, NV

Stan Robinson
Mannington, WV

Mandy Thorne
Mannington, WV

Marti Tomko
Westminster, MD

Jim Trogden - Rittman, OH

Torri Weed - Stonington, ME

Gene Winegart - Shreveport, LA

Dawn Wise - Peru, ME

Paula Wright - Gray, GA

This work is based upon work supported by the National Science Foundation under Grant No. 9353035 with additional support from the Chevron Corporation. Any opinions, findings, and conclusions or recommendations expressed in this publication are those of the authors and do not necessarily reflect the views of the National Science Foundation or the Chevron Corporation. Any mention of trade names does not imply endorsement from the National Science Foundation or the Chevron Corporation.

Table of Contents

Introducing Oceans . . . . Oxi

Why Are Oceans Important? . . . . Oxii

Investigation 1: The Properties of Seawater O1
The Properties of Seawater O5

Investigation 2: Ocean Waves O9
Waves and Wave Properties O14

Investigation 3: Ocean Currents and Circulation . . O19
Ocean Currents O24

Investigation 4: Mapping the Ocean Floor O29
The Ocean Floor O36

Investigation 5: Changes in the Ocean Floor O39
Plate Tectonics O43

Investigation 6: Adaptations to the Ocean O47
Adapting to Life in the Ocean O54

Investigation 7: Investigating a Place in the Ocean . O59

Reflecting O63

The Big Picture O64

Glossary O65

Using Investigating Earth Systems

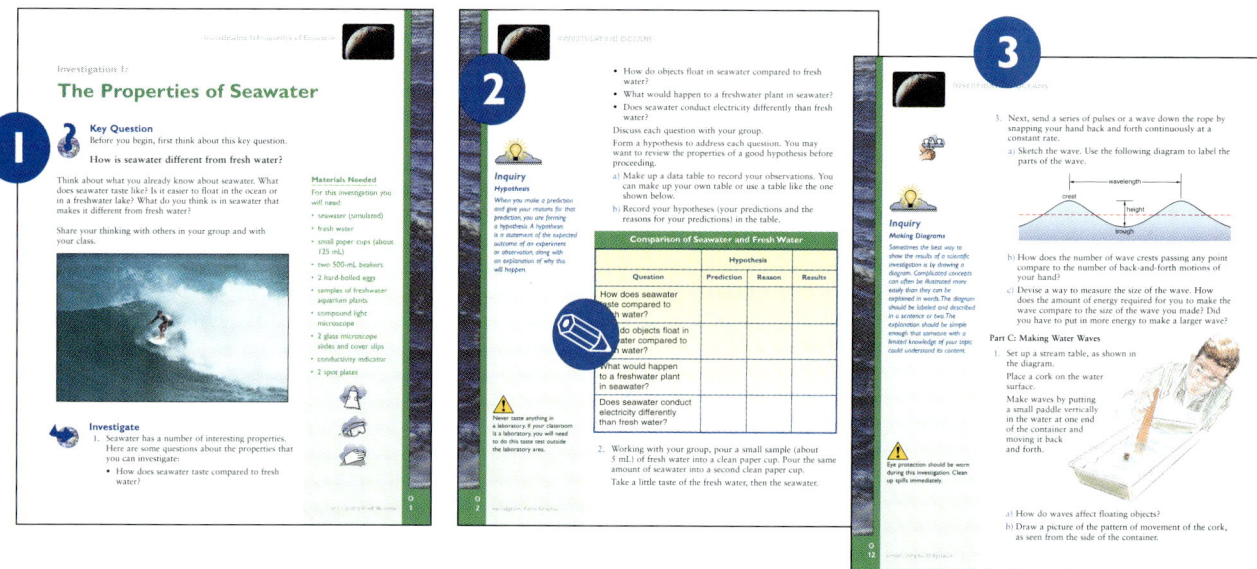

Look for the following features in this module to help you learn about the Earth system.

1. Key Question

Before you begin, you will be asked to think about the key question you will investigate. You do not need to come up with a correct answer. Instead you will be expected to take some time to think about what you already know. You can then share your ideas with your small group and with the class.

2. Investigate

Geoscientists learn about the Earth system by doing investigations. That is exactly what you will be doing. Sometimes you will be given the procedures to follow. Other times you will need to decide what question you want to investigate and what procedure to follow.

3. Inquiry

You will use inquiry processes to investigate and solve problems in an orderly way. Look for these reminders about the processes you are using.

Throughout your investigations you will keep your own journal. Your journal is like one that scientists keep when they investigate a scientific question. You can enter anything you think is important during the investigation. There will also be questions after many of the **Investigate** steps for you to answer and enter in your journal. You will also need to think about how the Earth works as a set of systems. You can write the connections you make after each investigation on your *Earth System Connection* sheet in your journal.

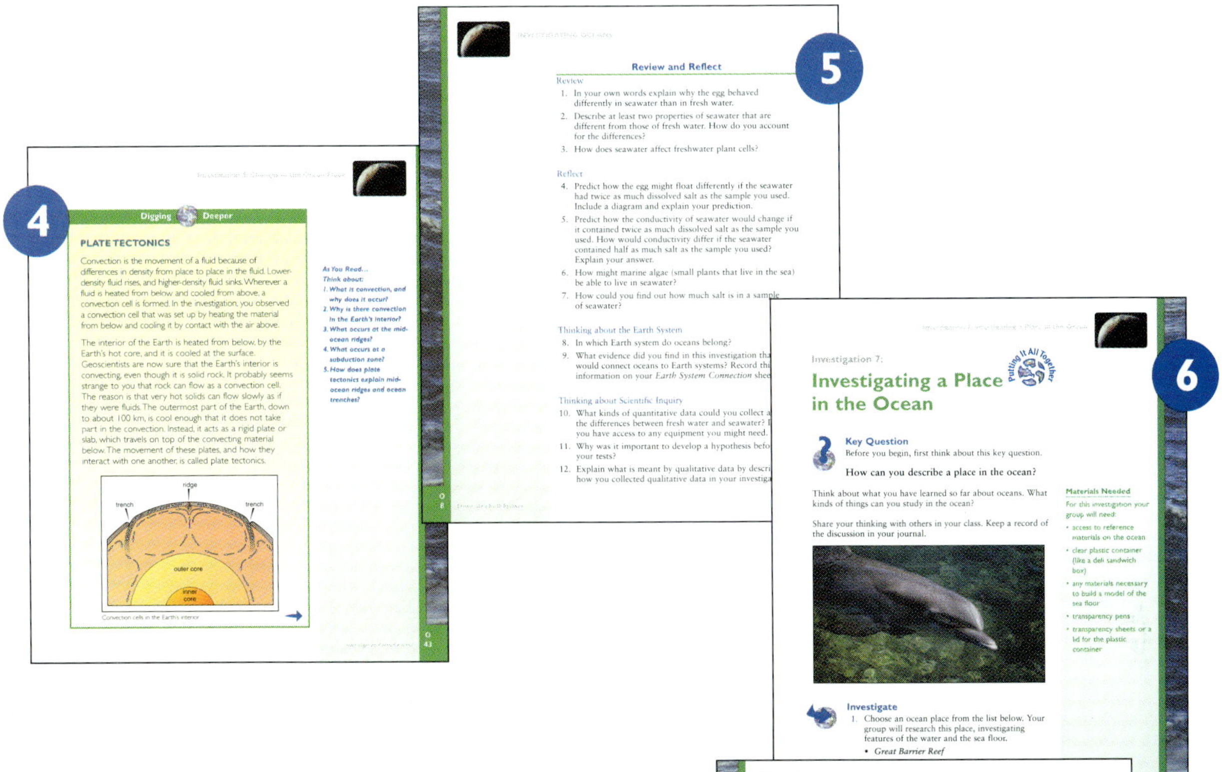

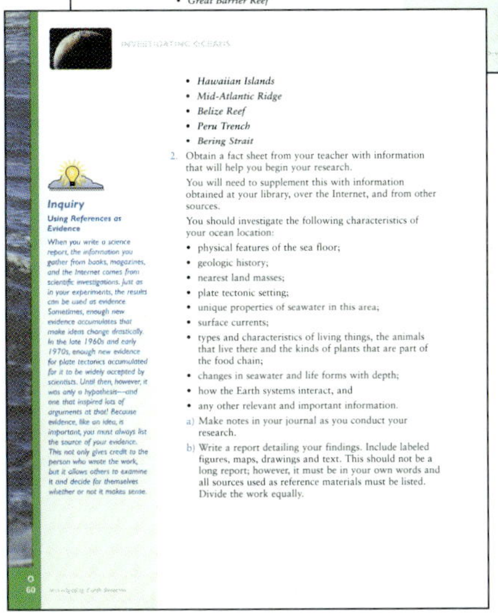

Review and Reflect

Review

1. In your own words explain why the egg behaved differently in seawater than in fresh water.

2. Describe at least two properties of seawater that are different from those of fresh water. How do you account for the differences?

3. How does seawater affect freshwater plant cells?

Reflect

4. Predict how the egg might float differently if the seawater had twice as much dissolved salt as the sample you used. Include a diagram and explain your prediction.

5. Predict how the conductivity of seawater would change if it contained twice as much dissolved salt as the sample you used. How would conductivity differ if the seawater contained half as much salt as the sample you used? Explain your answer.

6. How might marine algae (small plants that live in the sea) be able to live in seawater?

7. How could you find out how much salt is in a sample of seawater?

Thinking about the Earth System

8. In which Earth system do oceans belong?

9. What evidence did you find in this investigation that would connect oceans to Earth systems? Record this information on your *Earth System Connection* sheet.

Thinking about Scientific Inquiry

10. What kinds of quantitative data could you collect about the differences between fresh water and seawater? If you have access to any equipment you might need.

11. Why was it important to develop a hypothesis before your tests?

12. Explain what is meant by qualitative data by describing how you collected qualitative data in your investigation.

Digging Deeper

PLATE TECTONICS

Convection is the movement of a fluid because of differences in density from place to place in the fluid. Lower-density fluid rises, and higher-density fluid sinks. Wherever a fluid is heated from below and cooled from above, a convection cell is formed. In the investigation, you observed a convection cell that was set up by heating the material from below and cooling it by contact with the air above.

The interior of the Earth is heated from below by the Earth's hot core, and it is cooled at the surface. Geoscientists are now sure that the Earth's interior is convecting, even though it is solid rock. It probably seems strange to you that rock can flow as a convection cell. The reason is that very hot solids can flow slowly as if they were fluids. The outermost part of the Earth, down to about 100 km, is cool enough that it does not take part in the convection. Instead, it acts as a rigid plate or slab, which travels on top of the convecting material below. The movement of these plates, and how they interact with one another, is called plate tectonics.

As You Read...
Think about:
1. What is convection, and why does it occur?
2. Why is there convection in the Earth's interior?
3. What occurs at the mid-ocean ridges?
4. What occurs at a subduction zone?
5. How does plate tectonics explain mid-ocean ridges and ocean trenches?

Convection cells in the Earth's interior

Investigation 7:

Investigating a Place in the Ocean

Putting It All Together

Key Question
Before you begin, first think about this key question.

How can you describe a place in the ocean?

Think about what you have learned so far about oceans. What kinds of things can you study in the ocean?

Share your thinking with others in your class. Keep a record of the discussion in your journal.

Investigate

1. Choose an ocean place from the list below. Your group will research this place, investigating features of the water and the sea floor.
   - Great Barrier Reef

Materials Needed

For this investigation your group will need:
- access to reference materials on the ocean
- clear plastic container (like a deli sandwich box)
- any materials necessary to build a model of the sea floor
- transparency pens
- transparency sheets or a lid for the plastic container

- *Hawaiian Islands*
- *Mid-Atlantic Ridge*
- *Belize Reef*
- *Peru Trench*
- *Bering Strait*

2. Obtain a fact sheet from your teacher with information that will help you begin your research.

   You will need to supplement this with information obtained at your library, over the Internet, and from other sources.

   You should investigate the following characteristics of your ocean location:
   - physical features of the sea floor;
   - geologic history;
   - nearest land masses;
   - plate tectonic setting;
   - unique properties of seawater in this area;
   - surface currents;
   - types and characteristics of living things, the animals that live there and the kinds of plants that are part of the food chain;
   - changes in seawater and life forms with depth;
   - how the Earth systems interact, and
   - any other relevant and important information.

   a) Make notes in your journal as you conduct your research.

   b) Write a report detailing your findings. Include labeled figures, maps, drawings and text. This should not be a long report; however, it must be in your own words and all sources used as reference materials must be listed. Divide the work equally.

Inquiry

Using References as Evidence

When you write a science report, the information you gather from books, magazines, and the Internet comes from scientific investigations. Just as in your experiments, the results can be used as evidence. Sometimes, enough new evidence accumulates that make ideas change drastically. In the late 1960s and early 1970s, enough new evidence for plate tectonics accumulated for it to be widely accepted by scientists. Until then, however, it was only a hypothesis—and one that required lots of arguments at that! Because evidence, like an idea, is important, you must always list the source of your evidence. This not only gives credit to the person who wrote the work, but it allows others to examine it and decide for themselves whether or not it makes sense.

---

4. Digging Deeper

Scientists build on knowledge that others have discovered through investigation. In this section you can read about the insights scientists have about the question you are investigating. The questions in **As You Read** will help you focus on the information you are looking for.

5. Review and Reflect

After you have completed each investigation, you will be asked to reflect on what you have learned and how it relates to the "Big Picture" of the Earth system. You will also be asked to think about what scientific inquiry processes you used.

6. Investigation: Putting It All Together

In the last investigation of the module you will have a chance to "put it all together." You will be asked to apply all that you have learned in the previous investigations to solve a practical problem. This module is just the beginning! You continue to learn about the Earth system every time you ask questions and make observations about the world around you.

The Earth System

The Earth System is a set of systems that work together in making the world we know. Four of these important systems are:

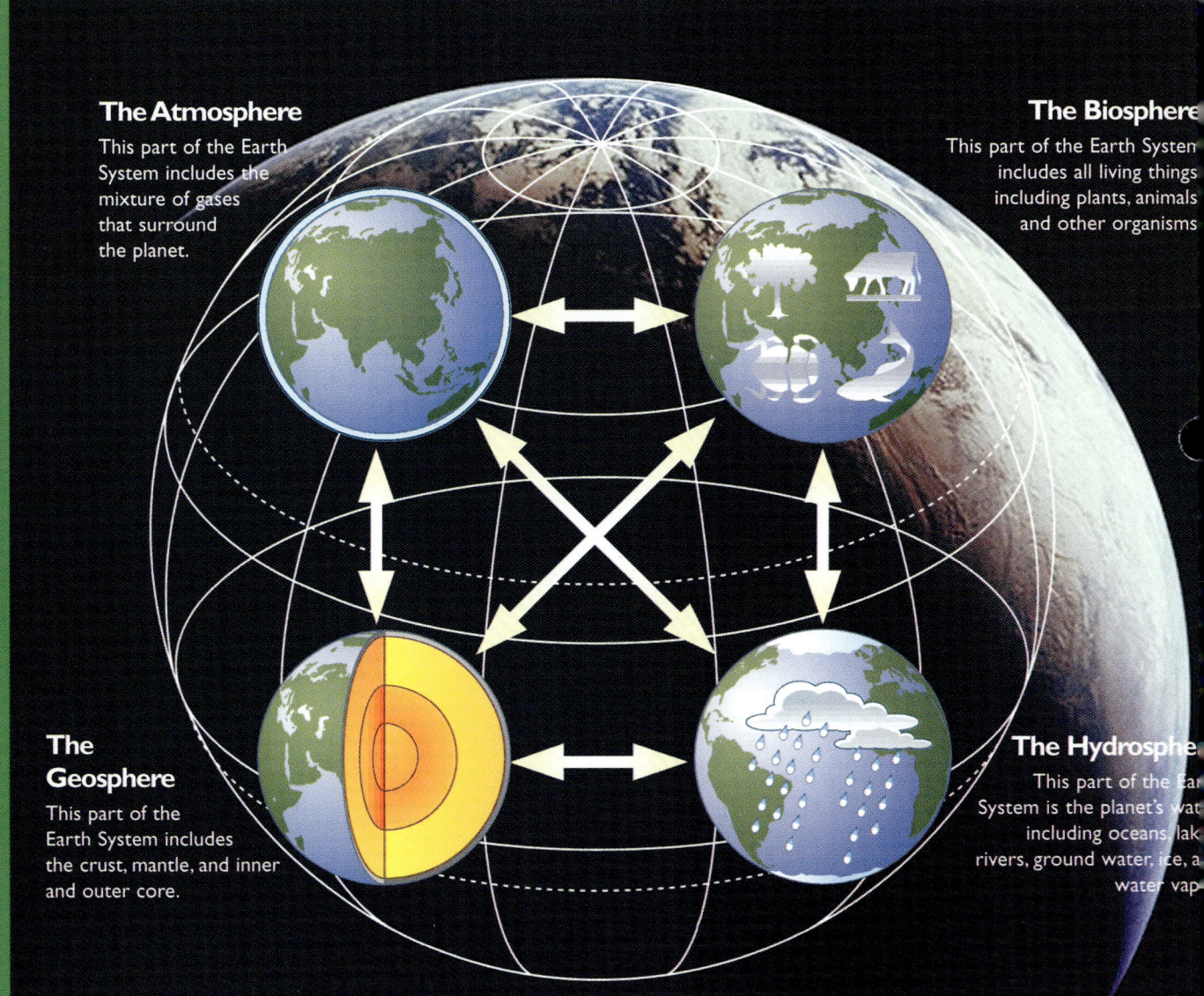

The Atmosphere
This part of the Earth System includes the mixture of gases that surround the planet.

The Biosphere
This part of the Earth System includes all living things including plants, animals and other organisms

The Geosphere
This part of the Earth System includes the crust, mantle, and inner and outer core.

The Hydrosphere
This part of the Earth System is the planet's water including oceans, lakes, rivers, ground water, ice, and water vapor

These systems, and others, have been working together since the Earth's beginning about 4.5 billion years ago. They are still working, because the Earth is always changing, even though we cannot always observe these changes. Energy from within and outside the Earth leads to changes in the Earth System. Changes in any one of these systems affects the others. This is why we think of the Earth as made of interrelated systems.

During your investigations, keep the Earth System in mind. At the end of each investigation you will be asked to think about how the things you have discovered fit with the Earth System.

To further understand the Earth System, take a look at **THE BIG PICTURE** shown on page 64.

Introducing Inquiry Processes

When geologists and other scientists investigate the world, they use a set of inquiry processes. Using these processes is very important. They ensure that the research is valid and reliable. In your investigations, you will use these same processes. In this way, you will become a scientist, doing what scientists do. Understanding inquiry processes will help you to investigate questions and solve problems in an orderly way. You will also use inquiry processes in high school, in college, and in your work.

During this module, you will learn when, and how, to use these inquiry processes. Use the chart below as a reference about the inquiry processes.

Inquiry Processes:	How scientists use these processes
Explore questions to answer by inquiry	Scientists usually form a question to investigate after first looking at what is known about a scientific idea. Sometimes they predict the most likely answer to a question. They base this prediction on what they already know to be true.
Design an investigation	To make sure that the way they test ideas is fair, scientists think very carefully about the design of their investigations. They do this to make sure that the results will be valid and reliable.
Conduct an investigation	After scientists have designed an investigation, they conduct their tests. They observe what happens and record the results. Often, they repeat a test several times to ensure reliable results.
Collect and review data using tools	Scientists collect information (data) from their tests. The data may be numerical (numbers), or verbal (words). To collect and manage data, scientists use tools such as computers, calculators, tables, charts, and graphs.
Use evidence to develop ideas	Evidence is very important for scientists. Just as in a court case, it is proven evidence that counts. Scientists look at the evidence other scientists have collected, as well as the evidence they have collected themselves.
Consider evidence for explanations	Finding strong evidence does not always provide the complete answer to a scientific question. Scientists look for likely explanations by studying patterns and relationships within the evidence.
Seek alternative explanations	Sometimes, the evidence available is not clear or can be interpreted in other ways. If this is so, scientists look for different ways of explaining the evidence. This may lead to a new idea or question to investigate.
Show evidence & reasons to others	Scientists communicate their findings to other scientists to see if they agree. Other scientists may then try to repeat the investigation to validate the results.
Use mathematics for science inquiry	Scientists use mathematics in their investigations. Accurate measurement, with suitable units is very important for both collecting and analyzing data. Data often consist of numbers and calculations.

Introducing Oceans

Have you ever wondered how and why storms develop over the oceans?

Have you ever wondered about the type of plants and animals that live in oceans?

Have you ever wondered how scientists study oceans?

Have you ever seen and heard ocean waves crashing against the shore?

Why Are Oceans Important?

If you dropped from outer space to a spot on Earth, chances are you would land in the ocean. Almost three-quarters of the Earth's surface is covered by ocean water. By size alone, the ocean is an important place to study. It is no coincidence that most of the world's population lives near water. The organisms that live in the ocean are an important source of food. Throughout history explorers sailed across the ocean to travel to "new" lands.

Other important features of the oceans may not be so obvious. Here are just two examples: The ocean regulates global climate by absorbing and releasing heat. Also, without processes that operate on the ocean floor, there would be no mountains. Understanding the processes that go on in the oceans will help you to appreciate how the oceans support life and shape the world.

What Will You Investigate?

Learning about the oceans will help you appreciate how important they are and how they fit into the Earth System. Here are some of the things that you will investigate:

- the properties of seawater;
- how ocean water circulates and how currents are formed;
- features of the ocean floor and how the ocean floor is mapped;
- how the ocean floor got its shape.

You will need to practice your problem-solving skills and be good observers and recorders as you work together with other members of your class.

In the last investigation, you will have an opportunity to apply all that you have learned about oceans. You will create a model of a place in the ocean that you could use to teach other students.

Investigation 1:

The Properties of Seawater

Key Question

Before you begin, first think about this key question.

How is seawater different from fresh water?

Think about what you already know about seawater. What does seawater taste like? Is it easier to float in the ocean or in a freshwater lake? What do you think is in seawater that makes it different from fresh water?

Share your thinking with others in your group and with your class.

Materials Needed

For this investigation you will need:

- seawater (simulated)
- fresh water
- small paper cups (about 125 mL)
- two 500-mL beakers
- 2 hard-boiled eggs
- samples of freshwater aquarium plants
- compound light microscope
- 2 glass microscope slides and cover slips
- conductivity indicator
- 2 spot plates

Investigate

1. Seawater has a number of interesting properties. Here are some questions about the properties that you can investigate:

   - How does seawater taste compared to fresh water?

• How do objects float in seawater compared to fresh water?

• What would happen to a freshwater plant in seawater?

• Does seawater conduct electricity differently than fresh water?

Discuss each question with your group.

Form a hypothesis to address each question. You may want to review the properties of a good hypothesis before proceeding.

a) Make up a data table to record your observations. You can make up your own table or use a table like the one shown below.

b) Record your hypotheses (your predictions and the reasons for your predictions) in the table.

Inquiry

Hypothesis

When you make a prediction and give your reasons for that prediction, you are forming a hypothesis. A hypothesis is a statement of the expected outcome of an experiment or observation, along with an explanation of why this will happen.

Never taste anything in a laboratory. If your classroom is a laboratory, you will need to do this taste test outside the laboratory area.

Comparison of Seawater and Fresh Water			
	Hypothesis		
Question	Prediction	Reason	Results
How does seawater taste compared to fresh water?			
How do objects float in seawater compared to fresh water?			
What would happen to a freshwater plant in seawater?			
Does seawater conduct electricity differently than fresh water?			

2. Working with your group, pour a small sample (about 5 mL) of fresh water into a clean paper cup. Pour the same amount of seawater into a second clean paper cup.

Take a little taste of the fresh water, then the seawater.

a) Discuss and record the major taste differences in your chart.

b) Look at the prediction you made. Do the results support your prediction? Explain.

3. Pour seawater into a 500-mL beaker. Pour an equal amount of fresh water into another 500-mL beaker.

Place one hard-boiled egg into the seawater, and another into the fresh water.

a) Observe the results and record your observations.

b) Look at the prediction you made. Do the results support your prediction? Explain.

c) What new question could you ask about seawater and its ability to support objects? How could you test your question?

⚠️ Eye protection should be worn during this investigation.

4. Using the low-power lens of a compound light microscope, observe the cells of a freshwater plant in seawater and in fresh water.

   a) Draw and label the cells that you observe.

   b) Record the results in your table.

   c) Look at the prediction you made. Do the results support your prediction? Explain.

5. Some substances conduct electricity better than others. You will use a conductivity indicator to determine how well electricity passes through fresh water and sea water. A diagram of a conductivity indicator is shown.

   Devise a way of recording your findings, either quantitatively (using numbers) or qualitatively (using words).

   Place drops of fresh water and sea water on the spot plates.

   Observe the conductivity of salt water and fresh water. Wash your hands after this investigation.

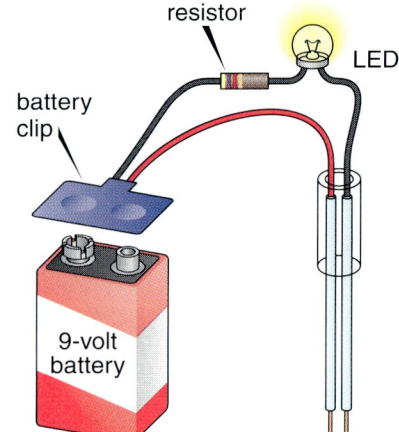

   a) Record your results.

   b) Look at the prediction you made. Do the results support your prediction? Explain.

Inquiry

Quantitative and Qualitative Observations

Observations dealing with numbers are called quantitative observations. An example of a quantitative observation is mass, recorded in grams. Qualitative observations refer to the qualities of the object. Color is often recorded qualitatively, as yellow, green, or blue, for example. Some observations can be made either quantitatively or qualitatively, depending on what tools are available and the level of accuracy needed for the test.

Disconnect the battery and remove the leads from the water when the conductivity indicator is not in use. Wipe up any spills immediately.

6. As a class, discuss the results of your tests. Did everyone have the same results? If not, explore reasons why your results may differ.

   Answer the following questions:

   a) Which results do all class members agree on? Which results are unclear or confusing?

   b) What new questions do you have after completing these tests?

   c) What new tests could you do? How else could you answer your new questions?

Digging Deeper

PROPERTIES OF SEAWATER
The Composition of Seawater

Seawater contains about 3.5% dissolved salts, by weight. If you let 100 g of seawater evaporate, and then you found the mass of the salts that were precipitated, you would have about 3.5 g of salts. The concentration of salts in seawater is called the salinity. The salinity is usually described in parts per thousand (about 35 parts per thousand).

A glass of water with table salt dissolved in it is very much like seawater. The difference is that many chemical substances are dissolved in seawater, not just the sodium and chloride of table salt. Most of them, however, are present only in very small concentrations. Several other substances, like calcium, magnesium, and sulfate, are also present in seawater.

Most of the substances dissolved in seawater are in the form of ions. An ion is an atom that has an electric charge, because one or more electrons have been added to the atom or taken away from it. Atoms of some chemical elements, like sodium, tend to give up an electron when they form ions. Because electrons have a negative electric charge, these ions are left with a positive charge. Atoms of other chemical elements, like chlorine, tend to take on an electron when they form ions. These ions are left with a negative charge.

Liquids conduct electricity only if they contain ions, which, because they have electric charges, can carry electricity by moving through the liquid. Pure water is not a good conductor of electricity because it contains only a very small concentration of ions. Seawater, with its abundant salt ions, is a much better conductor.

As You Read...
Think about:
1. *How is a glass of water with table salt dissolved in it similar to seawater? How is it different?*
2. *Why is seawater a better conductor of electricity than fresh water?*
3. *Why is the ocean "salty?"*
4. *Which is more dense, fresh water or seawater? Why?*
5. *What problem does seawater present for the cells of animals and plants that live in the ocean?*

Why Is the Ocean Salty?

Geoscientists know that the oceans have been salty for at least the past billion years of geologic time, because they observe salt deposits, called evaporites, formed by evaporation of seawater. How are evaporites formed? Imagine a bay that is partly sealed off from the open ocean, in a region with little rainfall. Seawater evaporates from the bay and is not replaced by rainwater, so more seawater flows in to take its place. But salts enter the bay along with the water, and the salts build up their concentration as the water evaporates. If their concentration becomes high enough, they are precipitated (the solids come out of solution) as small crystals, which sink to the bottom to form evaporite sediment. Most evaporites consist of the mineral halite (sodium chloride), which is mined for table salt, or gypsum (calcium sulfate), which is mined to make plaster and wallboard. In some places, evaporating ponds have been set up along the coastline to collect sea salt for human use.

The salts in the ocean come from two kinds of places. Rocks on land are broken down by weathering, and some of the rock material becomes dissolved in water as ions. The ions are carried to the ocean by rivers. Also, in certain places on the deep ocean bottom, hot springs emit water that is very rich in dissolved materials from deep in the Earth. These two processes have been acting through geologic time to make the oceans salty.

The Density of Seawater

The density of a material is its mass per unit volume. The mass of one cubic centimeter of fresh water is almost exactly one gram. Thus, the density of fresh water is almost $1 g/cm^3$. Seawater is slightly denser than fresh water,

because it contains so much dissolved material. When a river carrying fresh water reaches the ocean, the fresh water flows out on top of the seawater, and it mixes with the seawater very slowly, by the action of wind and waves.

The density of seawater varies slightly from place to place. Part of the reason is that the salinity varies slightly, either because the seawater is diluted with fresh water from rivers or rainfall, or because it becomes more concentrated by evaporation at the sea surface. Another reason is that, like most materials, seawater expands slightly when heated and shrinks slightly when cooled. Because the temperature of seawater differs from place to place, the density also varies. You will see later that these small differences are very important in causing ocean currents.

Plants and Animals in the Ocean

Plants and animals that live in the ocean range from very simple single-celled organisms like bacteria and algae to large multi-celled organisms like whales. On land, animals must protect their cells from the damaging effects of the atmosphere with skin or other coverings. In the oceans this is not a problem.

However, just as with animals on land, the liquids in the cells of animals in the ocean are not as salty as the surrounding seawater. However, the cells must still preserve their chemistry from the high amounts of salt in the seawater. They do this by complicated processes that keep the chemistry of the fluid inside the cell membrane stable.

Review and Reflect

Review

1. In your own words explain why the egg behaved differently in seawater than in fresh water.

2. Describe at least two properties of seawater that are different from those of fresh water. How do you account for the differences?

3. How does seawater affect freshwater plant cells?

Reflect

4. Predict how the egg might float differently if the seawater had twice as much dissolved salt as the sample you used. Include a diagram and explain your prediction.

5. Predict how the conductivity of seawater would change if it contained twice as much dissolved salt as the sample you used. How would conductivity differ if the seawater contained half as much salt as the sample you used? Explain your answer.

6. How might marine algae (small plants that live in the sea) be able to live in seawater?

7. How could you find out how much salt is in a sample of seawater?

Thinking about the Earth System

8. In which Earth system do oceans belong?

9. What evidence did you find in this investigation that would connect oceans to Earth systems? Record this information on your *Earth System Connection* sheet.

Thinking about Scientific Inquiry

10. What kinds of quantitative data could you collect about the differences between fresh water and seawater? Imagine you have access to any equipment you might need.

11. Why was it important to develop a hypothesis before your tests?

12. Explain what is meant by qualitative data by describing how you collected qualitative data in your investigation.

Investigation 2:

Ocean Waves

Key Question

Before you begin, first think about this key question.

What are ocean waves and how are they formed?

Think about what you know about ocean waves. What causes waves in an ocean? Are there different kinds of waves? How do ocean waves affect living and nonliving things?

Share your thinking with others in your group and with your class. Make a list that combines what you know about ocean waves with questions that you might be able to answer in this investigation. Keep your list for review later.

Materials Needed

For this investigation your group will need:

- 0.5 m piece of yarn
- 7 m (23 ft.) piece of rope
- stopwatch
- bag of marbles
- meter stick
- piece of chalk
- sand
- small, wooden paddle
- cork (or other floating object)
- smooth, hard, level floor surface
- stream table or similar container

Investigate

Part A: Observing Waves

1. Work with your group. Use photographs A and B on page O10 to answer the following questions in your journal:

A

B

a) What do you see happening in photographs A and B?

b) How do the waves change as they approach shore?

c) What do you think causes them to behave this way?

2. Look at photographs C and D and answer the following questions in your journal:

C

D

a) Describe two ways that the waves shown in photographs C and D are different?

b) Which would be more destructive to the shoreline?

c) What do you think caused these waves to be so different?

Part B: Properties of Waves

1. Stretch out a piece of rope 7 m (23 ft.) long on the floor.

One student should hold down one end of the rope while another student snaps the other end sharply sideways, parallel to the floor.

Be sure to hold the end of the rope tightly. Make sure you are ready before a student sends a pulse down the rope.

a) Describe how the pulse or disturbance travels along the rope.

b) Look at only one part of the rope. (You may wish to tie a piece of colored yarn in place to observe.) How does that part of the rope move as the disturbance passes by?

c) What happens to the pulse or disturbance when it reaches the other end?

2. Send some pulses of different sizes and shapes down the rope.

Use a stopwatch to time how long it takes a pulse to travel the length of the rope. Do this for pulses of several different sizes.

a) Does the speed of a pulse depend on the size of the pulse? If so, how?

Inquiry

Making Diagrams

Sometimes the best way to show the results of a scientific investigation is by drawing a diagram. Complicated concepts can often be illustrated more easily than they can be explained in words. The diagram should be labeled and described in a sentence or two. The explanation should be simple enough that someone with a limited knowledge of your topic could understand its content.

Eye protection should be worn during this investigation. Clean up spills immediately.

3. Next, send a series of pulses or a wave down the rope by snapping your hand back and forth continuously at a constant rate.

   a) Sketch the wave. Use the following diagram to label the parts of the wave.

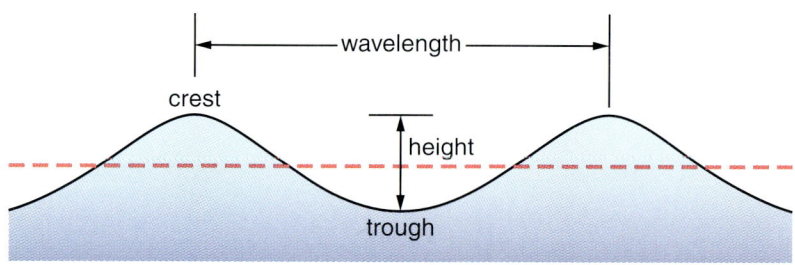

   b) How does the number of wave crests passing any point compare to the number of back-and-forth motions of your hand?

   c) Devise a way to measure the size of the wave. How does the amount of energy required for you to make the wave compare to the size of the wave you made? Did you have to put in more energy to make a larger wave?

Part C: Making Water Waves

1. Set up a stream table, as shown in the diagram.

   Place a cork on the water surface.

   Make waves by putting a small paddle vertically in the water at one end of the container and moving it back and forth.

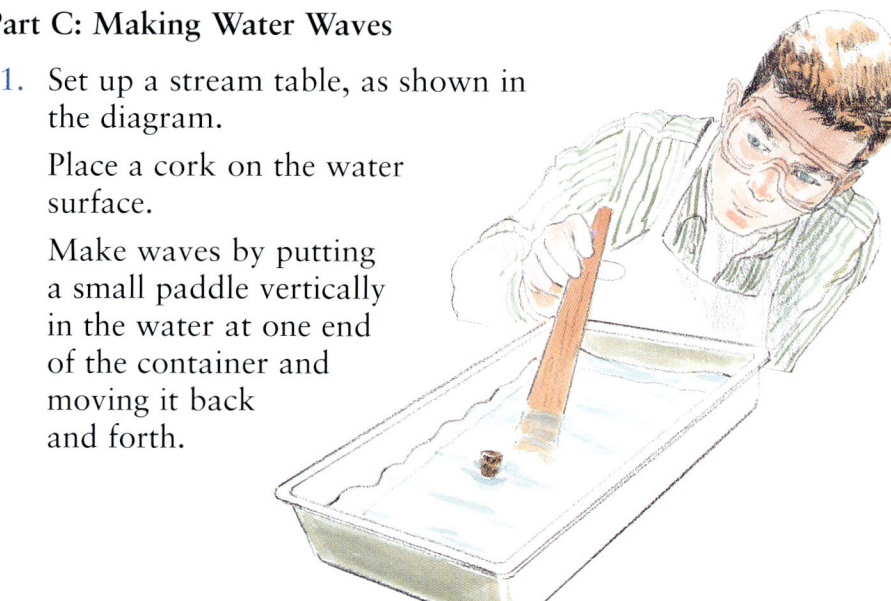

   a) How do waves affect floating objects?

   b) Draw a picture of the pattern of movement of the cork, as seen from the side of the container.

2. Remove the cork and continue to gently create waves.

   Observe the waves as they move against the other end of the container.

   a) Record your observations in your journal.

3. Add sand to the stream table so that there is a long, sloping "beach" at the end opposite from where you make the waves.

   Repeat the process of making waves, using the same amount of force as before.

   a) How are the waves different from when there is no sand beach?

   b) Explain the differences you observe.

4. Share your results with the rest of the class.

   a) Compare diagrams of the waves. What do they show?

   b) Discuss the action of waves. How do they affect floating objects? What is the difference in behavior of the waves when they meet a solid wall versus when they meet a sand beach?

   c) Moving the paddle supplied energy to make waves. In the ocean, where does the energy needed to make waves come from?

Part D: Wave Speed, Wave Period, and Wavelength

1. Make a straight chalk mark on the floor.

   One student with the stopwatch calls out the time every two seconds.

   A second student rolls marbles, one at a time, away from the chalk line.

   A third student uses a meter stick lying on the floor along the path of the marbles to estimate the spacing between successive marbles as they pass by.

   Repeat these steps four or five times. Vary the initial speed of the marbles from very slow (a few centimeters per second) to as much as a meter per second.

Inquiry

Modeling

You are using a stream table to model the action of waves on a sloping beach. Models are very useful scientific tools. Scientists use models to simulate real-world events and processes. They do this when it is difficult to study the real thing in a controlled way. It is important that you try to model what happens in the real world as accurately as possible.

Wash your hands after working with the stream table.

Be sure to pick up all the marbles that are used.

The speed of the marbles models the speed of water waves. The two-second interval between rolling the marbles models the wave period. The speed at which the marbles are rolled models the wave speed.

a) Describe in your journal how the spacing between successive marbles depends on the speed of the marbles.

b) Judging by your results, how do you expect the wavelength of ocean waves to depend on the wave speed, for a given wave period?

Digging   Deeper

WAVES AND WAVE PROPERTIES
What is a Wave?

A wave is a motion that travels through a material and carries energy from one place to another. Some common kinds of waves in nature are sound waves, light waves, and water waves. Waves are produced when a material is somehow disturbed. The motion made by the disturbance is transferred away from the area of the disturbance. The motion at one place in the material causes motion of the material next to it, and then that motion causes motion of more material, and so on.

When wind blows over a water surface, it makes waves. How wind makes waves is complicated, although it is easy to watch. Three factors determine the size of the waves: the speed of the wind, the time the wind has to act on the water, and the distance (called the fetch) the wind can blow over the water. When you stand at the seashore facing the ocean with a strong wind at your back, you can see the effect of the fetch. The waves start out small near the shore, but they get bigger when they are a distance from shore. The largest waves are produced by a strong wind that blows for a long time over a long distance of the ocean surface.

As You Read...
Think about:

1. What is a wave?
2. How are very large ocean waves produced?
3. How does the ocean and atmosphere interact to create waves? Refer to kinetic and potential energy.
4. What happens to the energy carried by a wave when it reaches the shoreline?

A long series of waves is called a "train" of waves. The crest is the highest point on the wave, and the trough is the lowest point. A train of waves is described by height, wavelength, period, and speed. The height is the vertical difference between a trough and a crest. The ratio of height to wavelength is called the steepness of the wave, as shown in the diagram. The biggest waves in the ocean have heights of more than 30 m! The wavelength is the distance from one crest to the next. Large ocean waves can have wavelengths of many hundreds of meters. The period is the time it takes two crests to pass the same point. Small water waves have periods of only one or two seconds, but very large ocean waves have periods of 10 to 15 s. The speed of the waves depends partly on wave size and partly on water depth. Large waves move faster than small waves.

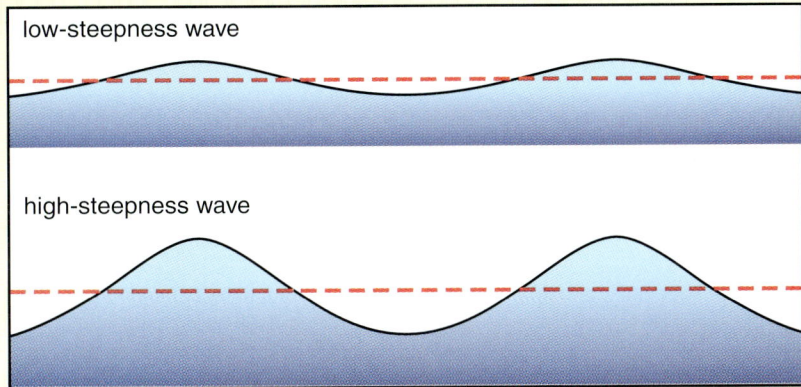

low-steepness wave

high-steepness wave

The Energy of Ocean Waves

Waves carry kinetic energy and potential energy. Kinetic energy is the energy of motion. Potential energy is energy associated with height. Think about dropping a heavy object on the floor. The higher you drop it from, the more energy it has, and therefore the more damage it can do when it hits the floor.

The wind puts some of its kinetic energy into the water waves, and that energy is then carried by the waves. Water waves have kinetic energy because the water is in motion while the wave passes by, and they have potential energy because of the difference in elevation between trough and crest. Large waves carry more energy than small ones, partly because the water motions are faster (more kinetic energy) and partly because there is a greater difference in elevation between crest and trough (more potential energy). It's important to remember that even though the energy is carried by the waves from place to place, the water itself returns to its original position after the waves have passed by.

Most large ocean waves are generated by winds in ocean storms. Winds in an ocean storm can be very strong and they can blow for a long time. Winds in storms usually blow in a circular pattern, so the waves travel away from the storm in all directions. Once a large ocean wave is formed, it can travel for many thousands of kilometers without losing much of its energy. When it finally reaches a shoreline, it expends all of its energy.

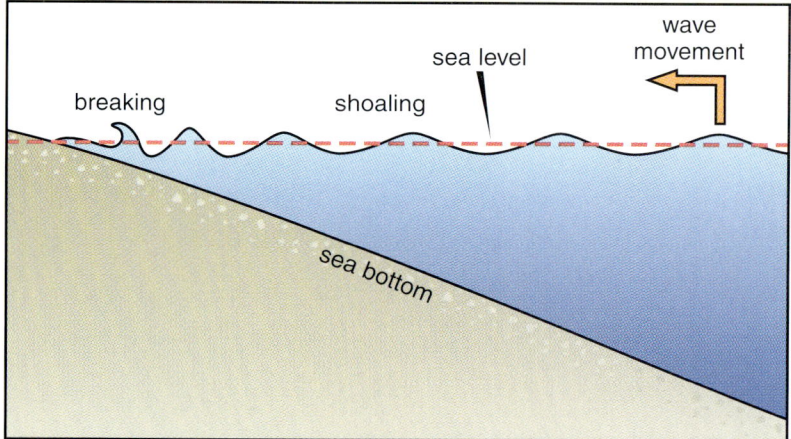

When waves approach a shoreline they slow down, because the speed decreases as the water becomes less

deep. As you learned in Part D of the investigation, the wavelength decreases as the waves slow down. The wave height, however, stays about the same. That means that the waves become steeper. Eventually they become so steep that they break, and the crest of the wave crashes forward onto the shore as in the diagram on the previous page.

When the wave breaks, it delivers all of its energy to the shoreline. All of this energy is converted into heat energy, in much the same way that friction converts the kinetic energy of a solid material into heat. In the process, however, the strong movements of water in breaking waves can do a lot of work. Water that moves up and down a beach moves sand and gravel and erodes sea cliffs. Water that crashes against rocky cliffs gradually breaks the rock into pieces and carries it away. Most of the world's shorelines are shaped by the action of breaking ocean waves.

Review and Reflect

Review

1. Draw a wave and label the wavelength, trough, crest, amplitude, and wave height.

2. What is the relationship between wave energy and wave height?

3. What is the relationship between wave energy and the distance between wave crests?

4. What determines the speed of a wave?

Reflect

5. How is wave energy measured?

6. Why do you think that large waves can travel for long distances across the ocean surface?

7. If you are floating in the ocean and waves pass by, how will your body move? Explain.

8. If a wave washes over you at the beach, how will your body move? Explain your answer.

Thinking about the Earth System

9. How are waves connected to the atmosphere?

10. Write any other connection that you have discovered in this investigation to connect ocean waves to the geosphere, hydrosphere, and biosphere. You can record this information on your *Earth System Connection* sheet.

Thinking about Scientific Inquiry

11. How did you organize data in this investigation?

12. Why was the use of models required in this investigation?

Investigation 3:

Ocean Currents and Circulation

Key Question

Before you begin, first think about this key question.

What causes ocean currents?

In the last activity you discovered that energy, not water, is moved by ocean waves. Think about what you know about how water moves. What is an ocean current, and how is it different from a wave? In what directions do ocean currents move?

Share your thinking with others in your group and with your class. Keep a record of the discussion in your journal.

Materials Needed

For this investigation your group will need:

• two 2-L bottles
• clear, rectangular container (5.6 L/1.5 gallon)
• supply of warm water
• two 400 mL beakers
• food coloring (blue, red, and green)
• ice
• 3.5% salt solution
• salt
• tablespoon

Investigate

Part A: Surface Currents

1. Examine the map of ocean surface currents shown on the next page.

   Look for any patterns you can see.

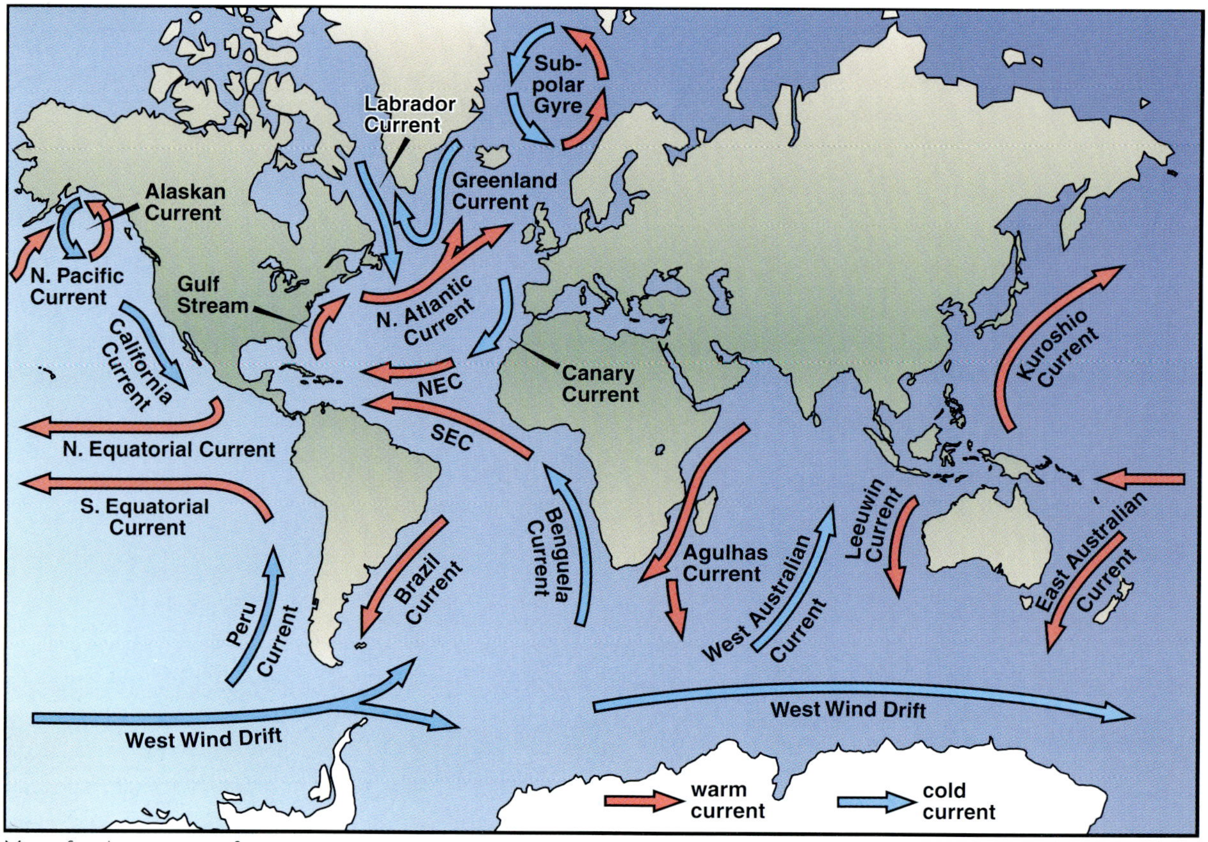

Map of major ocean surface currents

Inquiry

Charts and Tables

Charts and tables organize lots of information in a small amount of space. They can be useful in interpreting information because they allow you to focus on the most important points.

a) Make a table that shows direction of the flow of the current (towards the Equator, away from the Equator, along the Equator, or along polar latitudes), source location (does the current flow from the pole or from the Equator) and the water temperature (warm or cold) for the Kuroshio, Peru, Benguela, Gulf Stream, West Wind Drift, and South Equatorial currents shown on the map.

2. Study the map and your table. Discuss the following questions with your group. Record your answers.

a) In general, do warm or cold currents flow away from the Equator?

b) Do warm or cold currents flow towards the Equator?

c) What is the general relationship between the source of a current and the temperature of the water in the current?

d) Is this relationship always true? Explain your answer using evidence.

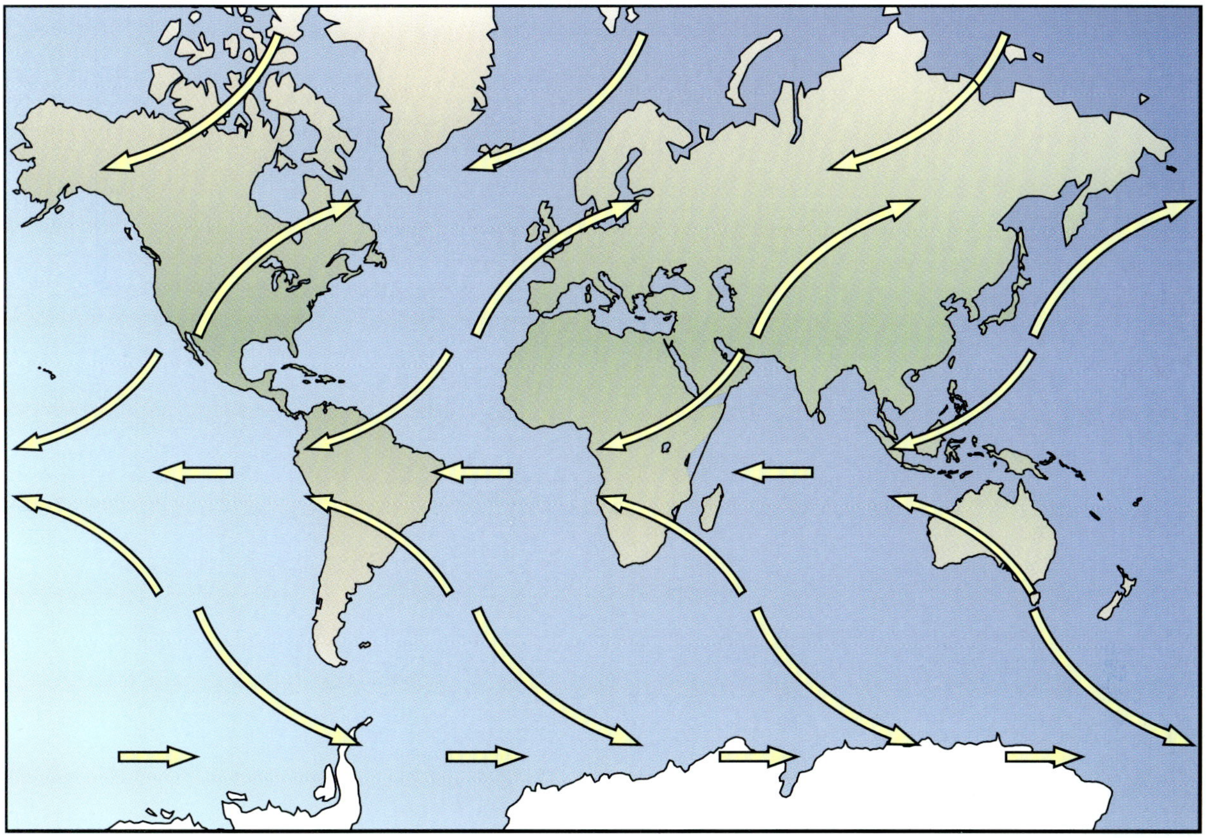

Map of major wind systems

3. Discuss your answers with your class.

   a) What patterns do you see between surface currents and wind direction?

   b) What new questions do you have?

   c) Form a hypothesis to explain the relationship between wind direction and surface currents. Give reasons based on evidence.

Part B: Deep Ocean Currents

1. Surface currents are not the only kind of ocean current. Before beginning the next part of the investigation, answer the following questions:

   a) Will "salty" water float or sink? Make a prediction of what you think will happen and explain your prediction. (You are forming a hypothesis.)

   b) Will warm water float or sink? Explain your answer.

Inquiry

Hypotheses and Theories

Scientists look for patterns and relationships. From their observations, they can predict whether the patterns will hold true in different situations. If the same patterns and relationships appear repeatedly, a hypothesis may reach the status of theory. A theory is a hypothesis that has never been disproven.

Inquiry

Controls and Variables

When evaluating experimental results, it is useful to have a basis for comparison. The control in an experiment is like a benchmark that you use to show differences caused by the addition of a variable or a change in a variable. In a controlled experiment, everything except the variable has to be kept the same. If not, it is impossible to know whether the variable caused the result, or if the change was caused by some other factor.

Use caution when working with hot water. Use water that is cool enough that it can be touched safely.

2. Fill two 2-L soda bottles with warm water.

   To one bottle, add five drops of green food coloring. This is the control.

   In the other bottle, add 30 mL (2 tbsp.) of salt before adding five drops of green food coloring.

   a) Record your observations in your journal.

   b) Describe any differences you observe in the way food coloring moves throughout the two bottles.

   c) Does this support your hypothesis? Explain.

3. Fill two 2-L bottles with cold water, leaving a small space at the top.

   In one of the bottles add more cold water. This is the control.

   In the other, slowly add hot water.

   Add five drops of green food coloring to both bottles, at roughly the same time.

   a) Record your observations in your journal.

   b) Describe any differences you observe in the way food coloring moves throughout the two bottles.

   c) Does this support your hypothesis? Explain.

4. Discuss the following with your group. Record your answers in your journal.

   a) If you added hot fresh water to fresh water at room temperature, would it float or sink?

   b) If you added cold salt water to fresh water at room temperature, would it float or sink?

5. You will now be given an opportunity to test your hypotheses.

   Fill a clear, rectangular container with room temperature tap water.

   In a 400 mL beaker, add 10 drops of red food coloring to 100 mL warm water (at least 50°C).

   In another 400 mL beaker, prepare 100 mL of very cold "seawater" (about 5°C). You will need ice to bring the temperature down. Color the very cold seawater with 10 drops of blue food coloring.

6. Slowly, pour the hot fresh water into one end of the container, using the inside wall of the container to slow the speed of the water.

   Allow the water to move throughout the container.

   a) Record observations in your journal.

7. Slowly, pour the cold seawater into the other end of the container, using the inside wall of the container to slow the speed of the water.

   Allow the water to move throughout the container.

   a) What patterns do you observe?

   b) How do you explain your observations?

   c) Do your observations agree with what you predicted would happen?

   d) How does this experiment model what goes on in the ocean?

   e) What flaws can you find with this model?

Eye protection should be worn during this investigation. Spills should be cleaned up immediately.

8. Using the same materials, design a new experiment with your group.

   Repeat the experiment, but try changing one of the variables.

   a) Before beginning, write the procedure you intend to follow.

   b) What is your hypothesis? (What is your prediction and what reason do you have for predicting this?)

9. With the approval of your teacher, carry out your investigation.

   a) Record your observations.

   b) Discuss the results with members of your group. Did the results support your hypothesis? Explain your results in your journal.

10. Use the map of surface currents from earlier in the investigation to answer the following questions:

    a) Are surface currents near the South Pole generally warm or cold?

    b) Are surface currents near the Equator generally warm or cold?

11. Discuss which continent would have cold water along its edge, and which continent would have warm water along its edge. Be prepared to defend your answer.

    a) Record your thoughts in your journal.

    b) If temperature was the only factor contributing to seawater density, how would water flow in the deep ocean? (Hint: How does cold water move? How does warm water move?)

12. Discuss where you think water would be the saltiest (most saline). Discuss where you think water would be less salty (least saline).

    a) Record your thoughts in your journal. Give a reason for your prediction.

    b) If salinity was the only factor contributing to seawater density, how would water flow in the deep ocean? (Hint: How does "salty" water move?)

As You Read...
Think about:
1. What are the sources of heat on Earth?
2. How is heat moved from one place to another on Earth?
3. Why is the ocean layered?
4. What is a gyre?
5. What drives deep ocean currents?

Digging **Deeper**

OCEAN CURRENTS
Movement of Heat on the Earth

What is the basic reason why there are winds in the atmosphere and currents in the ocean? The Sun warms the Earth's surface by the sunshine you can see. The Earth radiates heat to outer space, although you can't see that with your eyes. On average, over the entire surface of the Earth, the heat added and the heat lost just about balance. However, areas at high latitudes lose more heat

to space than they gain from the Sun, and areas at low latitudes lose less heat to space than they gain from the Sun. Therefore, to keep the balance, heat has to be moved from low latitudes to high latitudes. This heat is moved partly by winds and partly by ocean currents. In the oceans of the northern hemisphere, warm currents tend to move to the north and cold currents tend to move to the south.

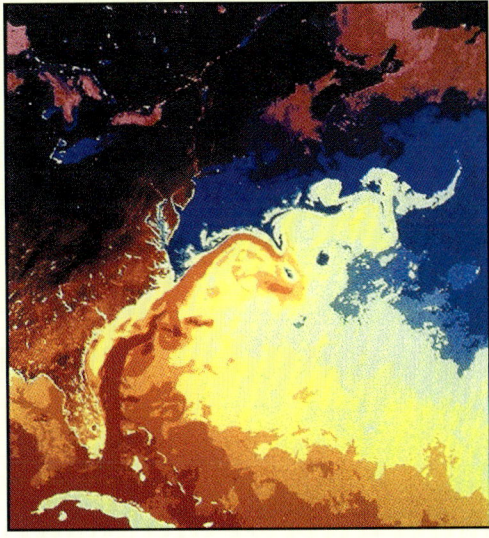

This thermal infrared image of the northwest Atlantic Ocean was taken from a NOAA satellite. The warmest temperatures (25°C) are represented by red tones, and the coldest temperatures (2°C) by blue and purple tones.

The ocean is layered. Except at high latitudes, the surface waters down to several hundred meters are warm. Below that, the water is very cold everywhere. The depth zone where the temperature changes from warm to cold is called the thermocline.

Another important fact about the ocean is that its width is far greater than its depth. A typical ocean is several thousand kilometers across and about four or five thousand meters deep. If the ocean were the size of a soccer field, the water would be only ankle deep! Keep that firmly in mind as you work with the oceans.

Currents in the Ocean

Mariners have always known that there are surface currents in the ocean. Some of these currents move faster than a meter per second, almost as fast as you can walk. The major surface currents are caused by the wind. In the previous activity you saw that when the wind blows over a water surface, it makes waves. The force of the wind on the water also moves the water forward to create a current.

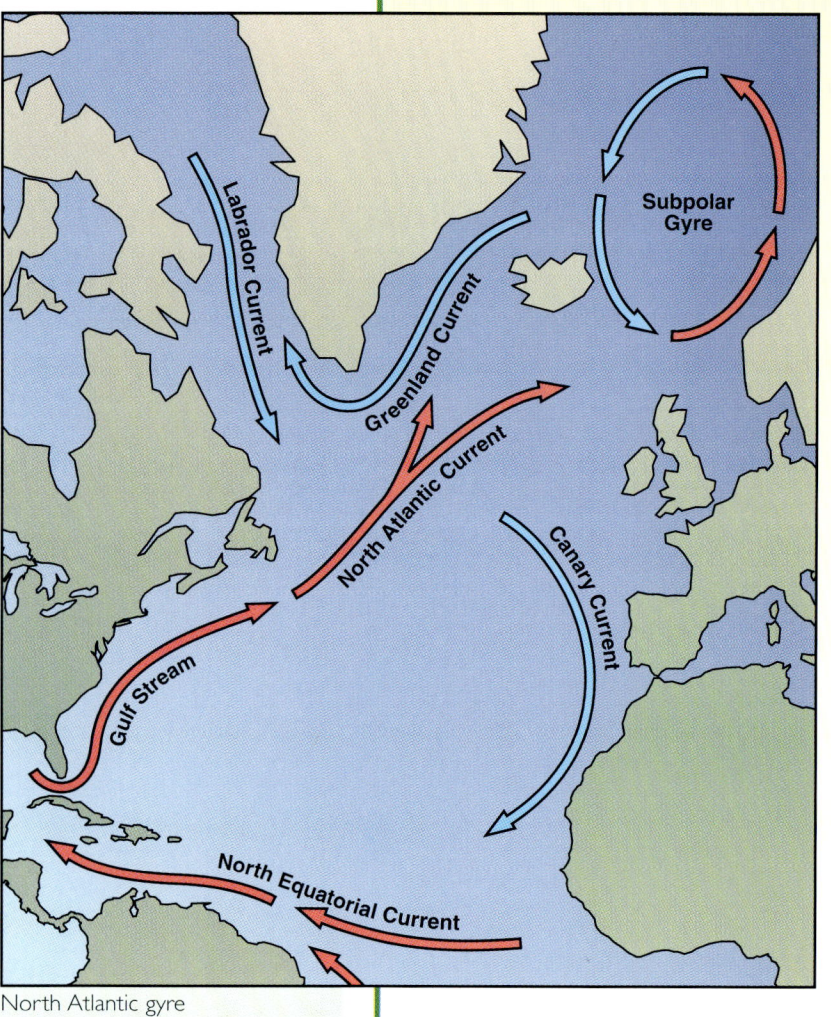

North Atlantic gyre

In each of the ocean basins of the northern hemisphere (North Atlantic and North Pacific), there is a loop of surface currents. In this loop, called a gyre, the currents flow clockwise around the center of the ocean basin. In the North Atlantic gyre, shown in the diagram, a warm current flows west just north of the Equator, then turns north to form the warm Gulf Stream off the east coast of North America. As the water moves north and then east around the northern edge of the basin, it is cooled, and a cold current flows south along the west coast of Europe and Africa to complete the loop.

Why do the gyres flow clockwise? The westward current in the low-latitude part of the gyre is driven by the trade winds, which blow very steadily from the east-northeast. The eastward current in the high-latitude part of the gyre is driven by the westerly winds, which blow irregularly from the west in the northern part of the basin.

Deep ocean currents are driven by differences in water density caused by differences in temperature or salinity, or both. They are much slower than surface currents, mostly only a few centimeters per second. Also, they are not as well known, because it is very difficult to measure such slow currents deep in the ocean.

All around the Antarctic continent, and in some places in the North Atlantic, surface water is chilled, increasing its density. Some of the surface seawater freezes. The ice contains less salt, so the water beneath becomes even saltier. This cold, salty water is more dense than water anywhere in the oceans. It sinks slowly and then flows along the ocean bottom for thousands of kilometers to the north. When it reaches low latitudes it rises up slowly to the surface and is warmed. It then flows back to the Antarctic region as part of surface currents, to complete the cycle.

Review and Reflect

Review

1. Does adding salt to water increase or decrease the density of water? Use evidence from the investigation to explain your answer.

2. How does the density of seawater depend on temperature?

3. How is heat moved from low latitudes to high latitudes on the Earth?

4. What causes surface currents in the ocean?

5. Where do most cold surface currents form? Where do most warm surface currents form? Explain.

Reflect

6. What evidence did you gather in your investigation that would explain the ocean currents shown in the map at the beginning of this investigation?

7. How realistic is the model you created for deep ocean circulation? Discuss both the strengths and weaknesses of your model.

Thinking about the Earth System

8. How do the hydrosphere and atmosphere interact to produce ocean currents?

Thinking about Scientific Inquiry

9. Why is it important to have a control in an experiment?

10. When did you form hypotheses in this investigation?

11. What is a variable?

12. What is the difference between a hypothesis and a theory?

Investigation 4:

Mapping the Ocean Floor

Key Question

Before you begin, first think about this key question.

How do you think we can find out how deep the oceans are?

Think about what you know about the depth of the ocean. Where is the ocean deepest? Where is it shallowest? How do scientists and ship captains know about the ocean floor?

Share your thinking with others in your class. Keep a record of the discussion in your journal.

Materials Needed

For this investigation your group will need:

- small and medium-sized rocks
- empty coffee can
- wire mesh (1 cm)
- string
- small weight
- metric ruler
- graph paper
- global map that shows the physical features of the ocean floor

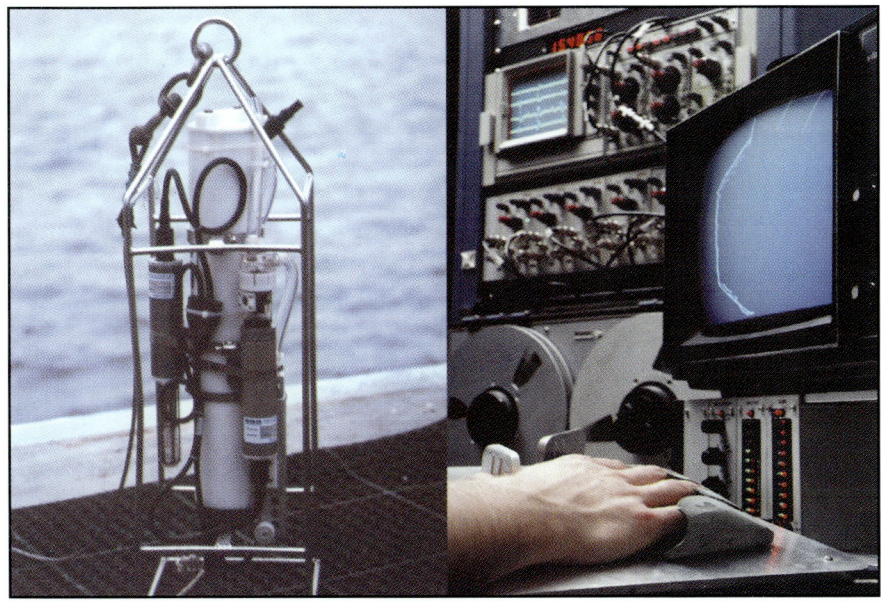

Investigate

Part A: Soundings

1. Imagine you are on a small ship. You have the job of mapping the bottom of a small bay to find out whether larger ships can use the bay. If the water

is shallow or if there are large obstacles a big ship could get stuck or damaged.

In your small group discuss what simple tools you could use to find out how deep the bay is.

Share your suggestions with the rest of the class.

a) Keep a record of this discussion in your journal.

2. Place some small and medium-sized rocks in the bottom of an empty can to represent an area of the bottom of the ocean.

Tie a small weight to one end of a string about 30 cm long.

Secure a wire mesh to the top of the can.

Your "sounding can" and "sounding line" should look similar to the one shown in the diagram.

3. Your challenge is to make a map of the floor of the sounding can, showing where rocks are located.

Before beginning, discuss how you can do this in an organized way.

Answer the following questions:

a) How can you use the wire mesh to guide your sounding line?

b) When you drop the sounding line, how are you going to tell someone where you took the measurements?

c) What measurements can you take that will help you locate the rocks?

d) How can you record your measurements so that you can figure out where the rocks are later?

e) Who in your group will be responsible for each of the tasks listed?

f) How can you present your findings so that the captain of a ship would know how to navigate through the obstacles?

4. Once your group has decided on its plan to map the floor of the bay, exchange your ideas with another group. Ask them to spot any problems with your plan. Do the same for their plan, if necessary.

a) When you have revised your plan, record it in your journal.

5. Follow your plan, taking soundings and recording their location and depth.

When you have taken enough measurements (at least 15), draw a map showing what the bay would look like if you could view it from above.

a) Include a copy of the map in your journal. Use labels that you think will help explain the drawing. Use colored pencils to help show features of the ocean floor.

6. Draw a side view of the ocean floor. This is called a cross section.

Lay out a line on a sheet of plain paper. Let that be the distance across the bay.

Plot points along that line showing the locations where you took depth soundings. If you did not take depth

Inquiry

Using Mathematics—Scale

Scientists use mathematics in their investigations. Accurate measurement, with suitable units, is very important when collecting data.

Scale is an extremely useful tool for geoscientists. Scale is used to compare the measurement on a drawing to the actual measurement of the object. In real life, soundings in a bay would probably be done in meters. These actual measurements would then be represented by a smaller measurement, such as a centimeter, on a drawing or map.

soundings along a straight line across the bay, it would be good to go back and do that now.

For each measurement point, measure a distance down from the line that represents your depth measurement.

When you have plotted all of the points, you can draw a continuous line that connects all of your plotted points. That line is a bottom profile of the bay. In general, profiles along different lines will look different. There is no "right" place to locate the line of your cross section.

a) Include the cross section in your journal. Label the deepest and shallowest points in the bay.

7. Share your results with the rest of the class.

Each group should explain the following points:

- What measurements were taken?
- How did you record your measurements?
- How did you turn the data into maps?

Discuss with the class how what you modeled in this part of the investigation could be used to find the depth of an actual small bay.

a) Record the results of your discussion in your journal.

Part B: Using Sonar

1. You just saw how much time and effort it took to map the floor of a very small bay using sounding. A more modern technique involves using an instrument to send a pulse of sound into the water and timing how long it takes the sound to bounce off the bottom and return. The instrument then displays the observation as a depth. This technique, called sonar (Sound Navigation Ranging), allows for quicker and more efficient mapping.

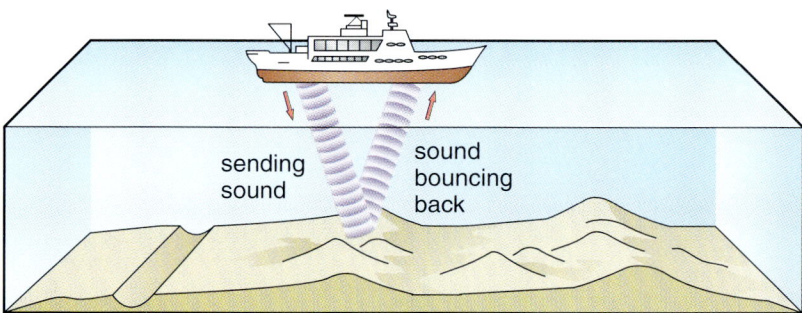

sending sound

sound bouncing back

a) In your own words, explain how sonar works.

b) What calculations must be done by the depth-sounding instrument to display the time for the echo to return as a depth?

2. You will now have the opportunity to see how sonar might be used to map the ocean floor. Pretend you are the captain of the marine research vessel *Catort*. You will be traveling west from Santiago, Chile to Sydney, Australia, taking soundings approximately every 1500 km. By making a line graph of depth as a function of distance traveled, you will be able to see what the ocean floor looks like in cross section. The ship started taking measurements at point 1, just a short distance off the coast of Chile. A table of data is shown on the next page.

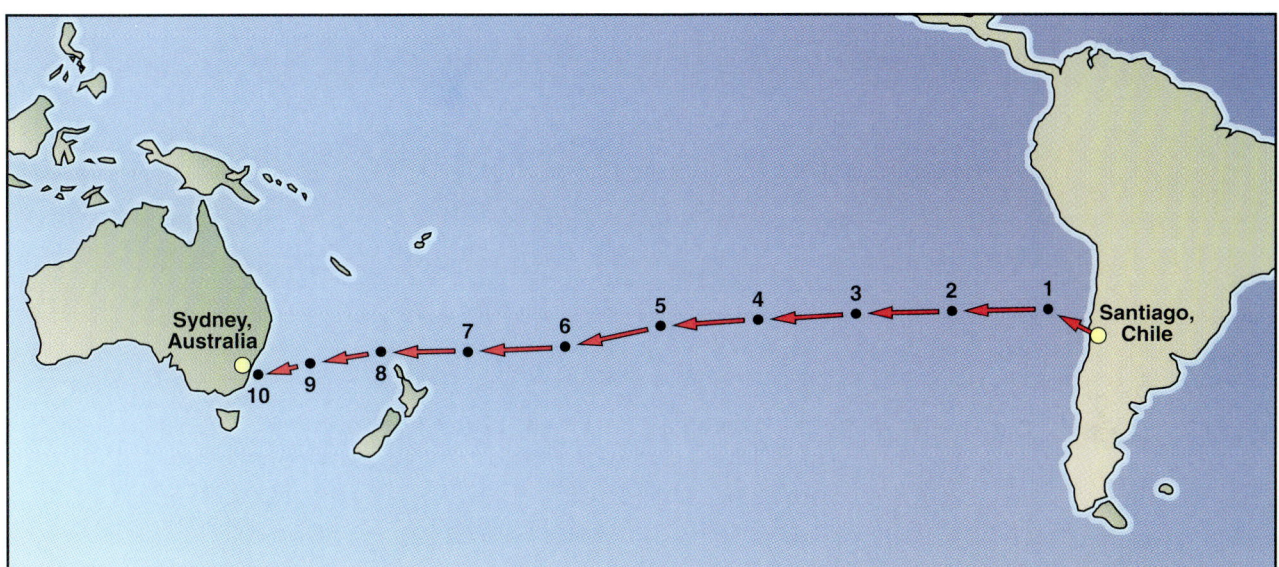

Data from the Voyage of the Marine Vessel *Catort*

Sounding No.	Approximate Travel Distance between Soundings (kilometers)	Sound Travel Time (seconds)	Distance the Sound Wave Traveled (meters)	Ocean Depth (meters)
1.	50	3.3		
2.	1450	5.0	7500	3750
3.	1500	3.7		
4.	1500	4.3		
5.	1500	2.2		
6.	1500	4.8		
7.	1500	5.7		
8.	1000	6.5		
9.	1500	1.3		
10.	1000	0.6		

Column 1 refers to the order of soundings taken as the *Catort* moved west to east. Column 2 indicates how many kilometers the ship traveled between soundings. Column 3 (sound travel time) shows the time it took for a signal to return to the vessel, after bouncing off the ocean floor. Column 4 shows the total distance traveled. In all, the vessel traveled approximately 12,500 km.

a) Copy the above data chart in your journal.

3. Sound travels at 1500 m/s. The total distance traveled by the signal equals the number of seconds times 1500.

Example: 5.0 s x 1500 m/s = 7500 m

Because the sound had to travel two ways (once to the bottom and then back up again), this number must be divided by 2 to get just the distance to the ocean bottom.

Example: 7500 m/2 = 3750 m

a) Using the example, complete the data chart with your group.

4. The map shows the voyage of a research ship.

The table gives the distance the ship traveled and the depths recorded.

Data from the Voyage of the Research Ship		
Sounding No.	Ship Travel Distance (kilometers)	Ocean Depth (meters)
1.	50	
2.	1500	
Etc.	....	

a) Use the data to draw a cross section of the sea floor. Graph paper will be helpful here.

5. Look at a global map that shows physical features of the ocean floor.

a) What does your picture show that is similar to the map?

b) What does it show that is different?

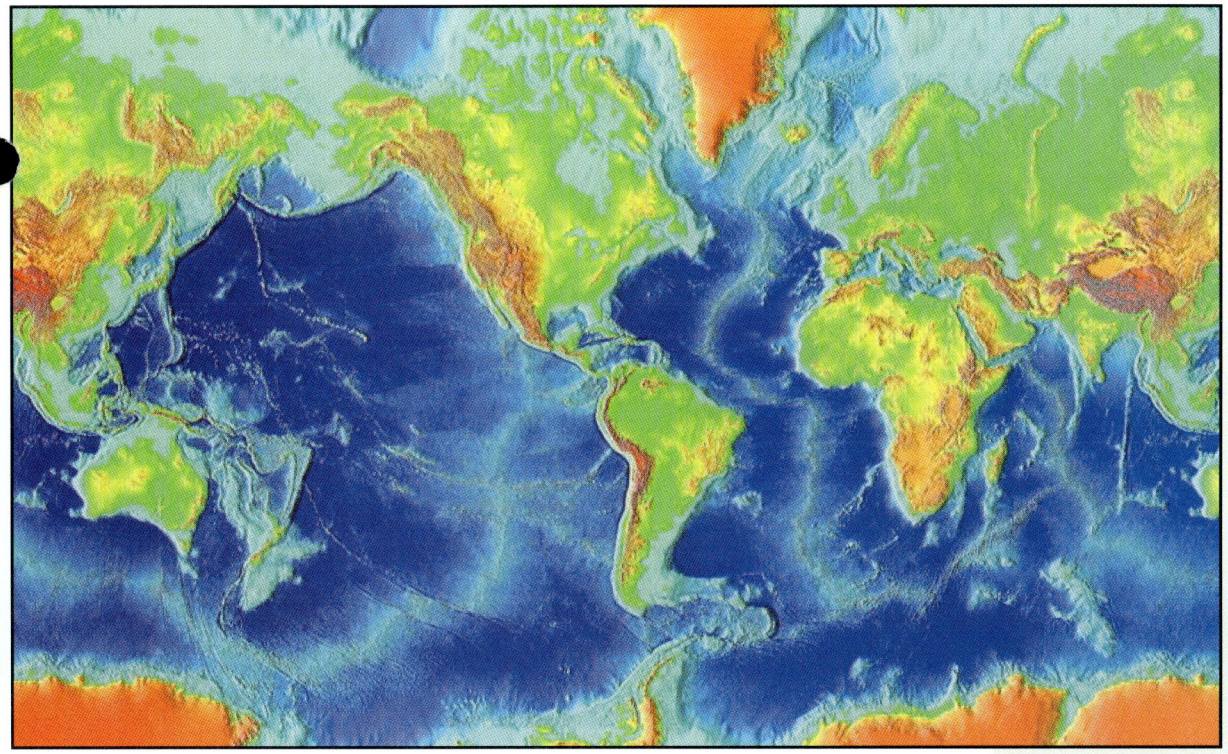

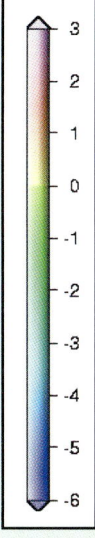

This key for the map shows elevation above sea level and depth below sea level in kilometers.

6. Compare your group's drawing of the ocean floor with that of other groups.

a) What problems did the other groups have in making a drawing from the data?

b) Did all groups have the same results? Why or why not?

As You Read...
Think about:
1. How were ocean depths measured before the 20th century?
2. How does sound travel?
3. How can sound be used to measure ocean depths?
4. What are the major topographic features of the ocean floor?

THE OCEAN FLOOR
Measuring Ocean Depths

It has always been a challenge to measure depths in the ocean. Before the development of sonar in the 20th century, the only way was to lower a heavy weight on a long rope or wire, as in your investigation. The problem with that technique is that it's time-consuming and difficult. Also, ocean currents push the weight and the wire sideways, causing the measurement to be somewhat inaccurate. Before the 20th century, oceanographers did not know much about the shape of the ocean floor.

Sound is a wave that travels through gases, liquids, and solids. Imagine that you have a long bar of metal or rock. If you hit the end of a long metal bar with a hammer, the material there is compressed. It then expands again, just as a rubber eraser returns to its original shape after you squeeze it. As the material expands, it compresses the material next to it, which then also expands, and so on. The result is a wave of compression and expansion that travels down the rod. Exactly the same thing happens when your vocal cords cause a vibration of the air. In water, sound waves travel at a speed of about 1500 m/s.

Sonar (the word comes from SOund NAvigation Ranging) is a technique that uses sound waves in the ocean for measuring distances, locating solid objects, and communicating underwater. The principle is simple.

Produce a pulse of high-frequency sound with an electrical device, and detect the echo of the sound after it bounces off a distant solid object. If the speed of sound in water is known, and the two-way travel time of the sound pulse is measured, the distance can be calculated. To detect objects like enemy submarines or schools of fish, the sound pulse is created as a narrow beam, and the beam scans a wide angle until the object is located by detecting an echo.

Measuring ocean depths using sonar is usually called echo sounding, and the instrument is called an echo sounder or a fathometer. (Ocean depths used to be measured in fathoms. A fathom equals six feet.) The sound beam is directed straight down, and the two-way travel time is measured. The device that creates the sound pulse is called a pinger, because you can hear the sound as a "ping"!

The Shape of the Ocean Floor

There are many kinds of topographic (surface) features, large and small, on the ocean floor. The diagram on the next page shows the major features of the ocean floor. All of the continents are bordered by wide areas, called continental shelves, where water depths are not much more than 100 m. Beyond the shelf edge, or shelf break, the ocean floor slopes down gently to the deep ocean. This sloping surface is called the continental slope. Most of the deep ocean floor, beyond the continental slope, is at depths of four to five kilometers. Some of these areas are irregular and hilly, but other large areas, called abyssal plains, are almost flat. In the middle of each of the world's major oceans is a broad ridge, called the mid-ocean ridge. Depths at the crest of the ridge are mostly only two to three kilometers. The very deepest parts of the ocean, with depths greater than 10 km, are long, narrow submarine valleys called ocean trenches.

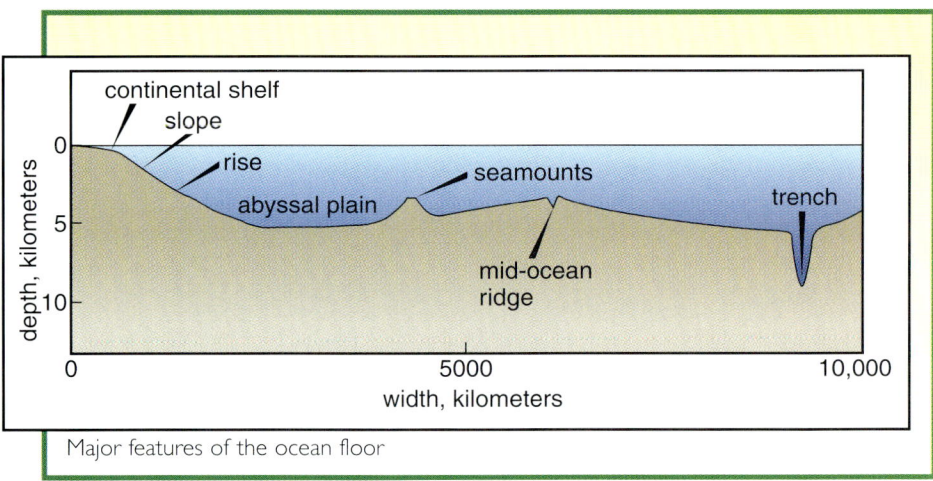

Major features of the ocean floor

Review and Reflect

Review

1. Describe two ways to measure ocean depth.

2. What is sonar?

3. How have changes in technology improved the accuracy of maps of the ocean floor?

Reflect

4. Which provides a more accurate reading, a sounding or sonar? Explain why.

5. Why is it important to map the ocean floor?

6. What are some of the problems involved in mapping the ocean floor?

Thinking about the Earth System

7. How does the depth of the ocean floor (geosphere) affect marine life (biosphere)?

Thinking about Scientific Inquiry

8. How did you use mathematics in this investigation?

9. Describe some of the similarities and differences between your model of sounding the ocean floor and a real-world setting in which soundings might actually be used.

Investigation 5:

Changes in the Ocean Floor

Key Question

Before you begin, first think about this key question.

How does the ocean floor get its shape?

Think about the profile of the ocean floor you constructed in the previous activity. How did it get its present shape?

Share your thinking with others in your class. Keep a record of the discussion in your journal.

Materials Needed

For this investigation your group will need:

• map of global topography

Investigate

1. To begin this investigation, you will watch a demonstration.

   A clear, heat-proof dish is half-filled with corn syrup.

   Four wooden blocks are placed on top of the syrup in the center of the dish.

The dish is then placed on a hot plate.

Before the hot plate is turned on, think about what might happen to the wood blocks.

a) Write a prediction about what you think will happen to the blocks.

b) Write a reason for your prediction.

2. When the hot plate is turned on and the corn syrup begins to warm, carefully watch what happens to the wood blocks.

a) Record your observations in your journal as a series of drawings.

3. Look at the prediction you made and the reason for it.

a) Can you accept your hypothesis or should you reject it? Explain your answer.

4. Discuss with your group what might have caused the ocean floor to look the way it does. As a group, keep a list of your ideas.

   a) Record the list in your journal.

   b) How does what happened to the wood blocks help to explain the features on the ocean floor?

   c) What could cause the ocean floor to form mountains and valleys?

5. Think about the demonstration with the corn syrup and wood blocks. Remember that things began to happen as the corn syrup heated up.

   a) What kind of event do you know that causes hot material to push through the Earth's crust?

   b) What kind of event happens when the Earth's crust breaks or moves suddenly?

6. Compare the map of global topography on page O35 with maps showing the occurrence of earthquakes and volcanoes on the following page.

   a) What do you notice about the relationship between earthquakes, volcanoes, and the shape of the ocean floor?

   b) How does the demonstration help explain the features of the sea floor?

   c) Propose a hypothesis to explain the features of the sea floor. Be sure to give a reason.

   d) Could similar processes happen on land? Why or why not?

7. Share your hypotheses with the rest of your class.

   a) Write any interesting hypotheses that you hear in your journal.

Inquiry

Using Maps as Scientific Tools

Scientists collect and review data using tools. You may think of tools as only physical objects such as sounding lines or echo sounders. However, forms in which information is gathered, stored, and presented are also tools for scientists. In this investigation you are using scientific tools: topographic maps and maps of earthquakes and volcanoes.

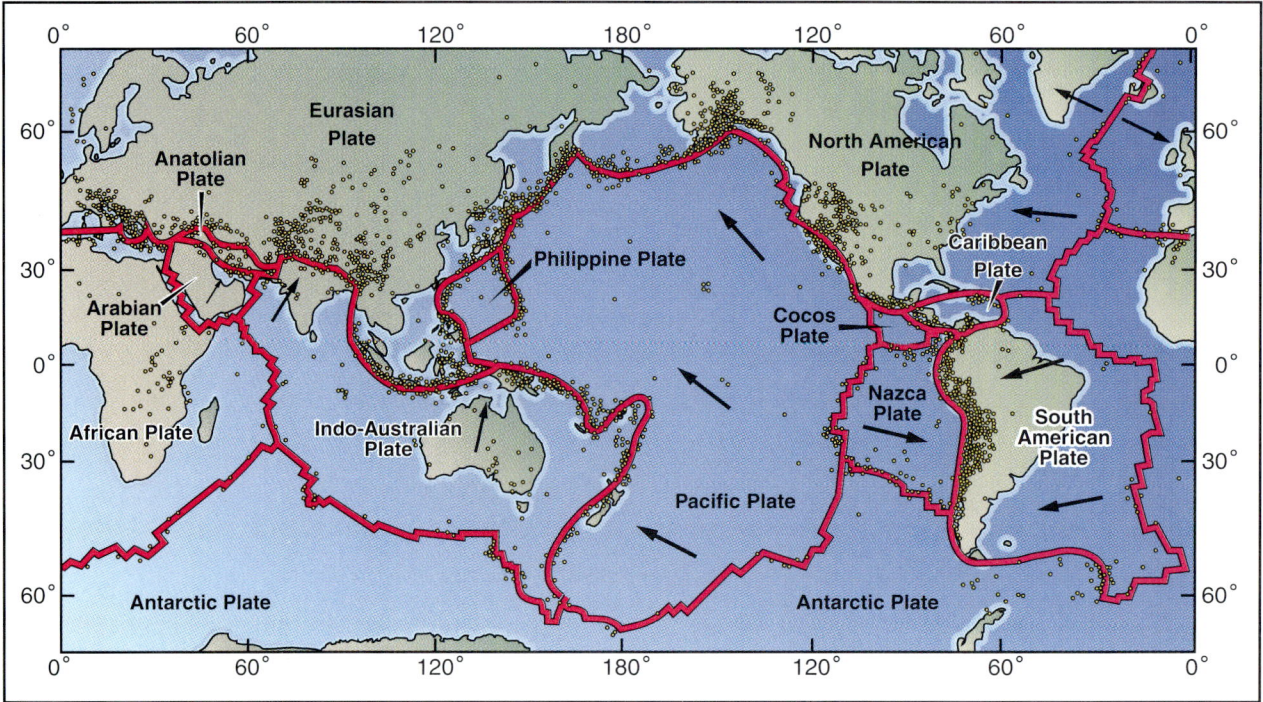

Map of earthquake occurrences

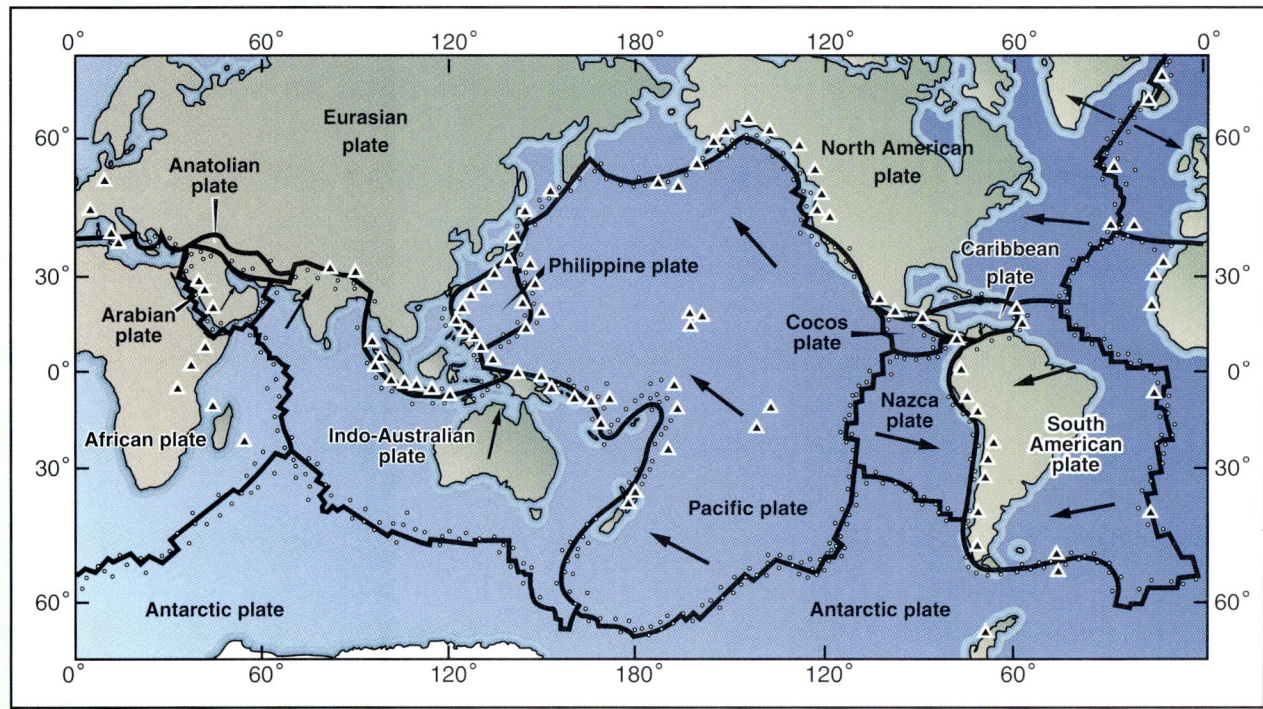

Map of volcano occurrences

Digging Deeper

PLATE TECTONICS

Convection is the movement of a fluid because of differences in density from place to place in the fluid. Lower-density fluid rises, and higher-density fluid sinks. Wherever a fluid is heated from below and cooled from above, a convection cell is formed. In the investigation, you observed a convection cell that was set up by heating the material from below and cooling it by contact with the air above.

The interior of the Earth is heated from below, by the Earth's hot core, and it is cooled at the surface. Geoscientists are now sure that the Earth's interior is convecting, even though it is solid rock. It probably seems strange to you that rock can flow as a convection cell. The reason is that very hot solids can flow slowly as if they were fluids. The outermost part of the Earth, down to about 100 km, is cool enough that it does not take part in the convection. Instead, it acts as a rigid plate or slab, which travels on top of the convecting material below. The movement of these plates, and how they interact with one another, is called plate tectonics.

As You Read...
Think about:

1. *What is convection, and why does it occur?*
2. *Why is there convection in the Earth's interior?*
3. *What occurs at the mid-ocean ridges?*
4. *What occurs at a subduction zone?*
5. *How does plate tectonics explain mid-ocean ridges and ocean trenches?*

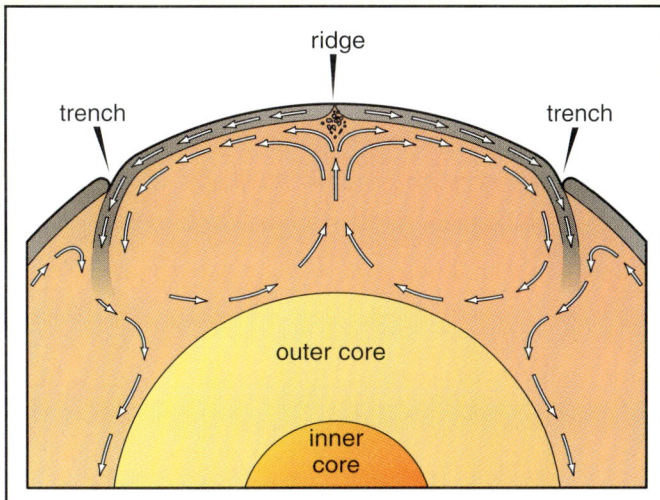

Convection cells in the Earth's interior

The upward-moving parts of the convection cells are under the mid-ocean ridges. Some of the rising material is melted on the way up, and it rises up to the crest of the mid-ocean ridge to form underwater volcanoes. All materials expand slightly when they are heated and shrink slightly when they are cooled. The mid-ocean ridges are high because they are warmer than the rest of the ocean floor, not because they are pushed upward from below. New plate material is formed on either side of the crest of the mid-ocean ridge, by submarine volcanoes. The two plates keep moving away from each other, at speeds of several centimeters per year.

The surface area of the Earth is not changing through time. If new plate material is continuously created at the mid-ocean ridges, it must be consumed at the same rate somewhere else. This happens in subduction zones. A subduction zone is a long belt on the Earth where one plate dives down beneath another plate at some angle. The place where the down-going plate first bends downward marks the location of an ocean trench.

As a plate goes down a subduction zone, it causes melting of the deep rock just above it. The melted rock rises up toward the surface, forming a chain of volcanic islands that parallels the ocean trench. The Aleutian Islands, west of Alaska, are a good example of a trench and a volcanic arc.

The oceans have not always looked the way they do today. As plates move around the Earth, they change the arrangement of continents and oceans. About 200 million years ago, all of the continents were joined together into a single giant continent, named Pangea. Later, Pangea split apart into several large pieces, probably because of a change in the pattern of convection in the deep Earth. The pieces drifted apart to form the Atlantic Ocean, the Indian Ocean, and the Antarctic Ocean. As these oceans have expanded, the Pacific Ocean has become smaller.

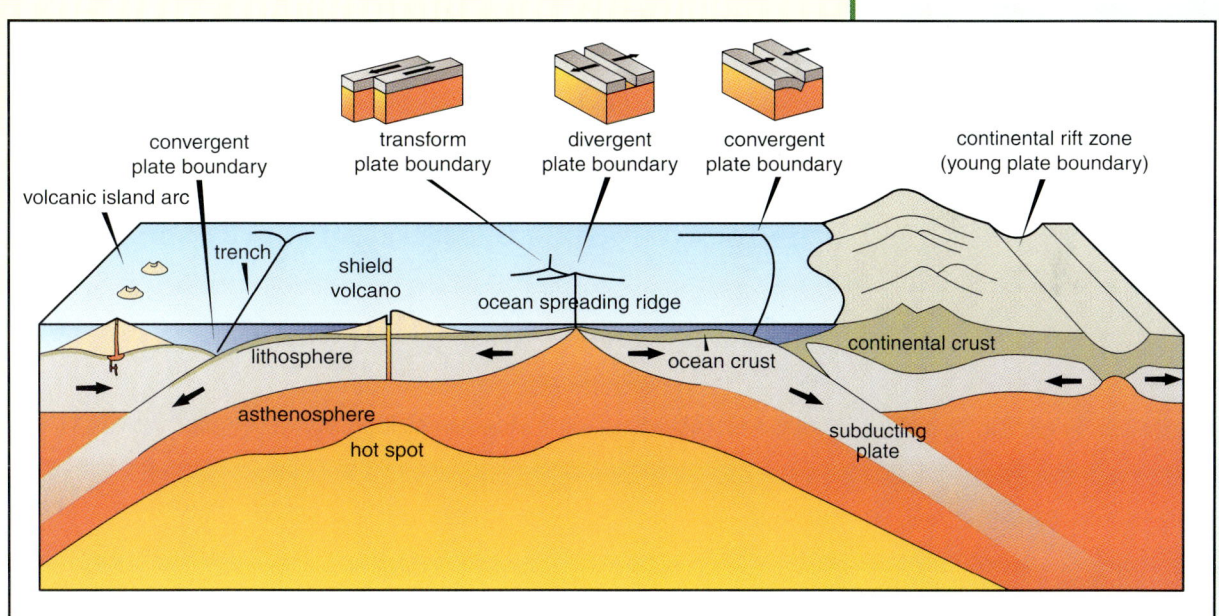

Review and Reflect

Review

1. Describe and explain the movement of the wooden blocks in the demonstration.

2. List the conditions necessary to cause convection.

3. What relationship exists between earthquakes, volcanoes, and the shape of the ocean floor?

Reflect

4. Refer to the Key Question: How does the ocean floor get its shape? Explain how the investigation has helped you answer this question.

5. What do you think the ocean floor would be like if plate tectonics were not operating?

6. What have you found out about the Earth's interior?

Thinking about the Earth System

7. How do changes in the geosphere affect the hydrosphere? What other connections to Earth's systems can you make? Record them on your *Earth System Connection* sheet.

Thinking about Scientific Inquiry

8. When did you make your hypotheses in this investigation? Give an example of a hypothesis you made and use evidence to explain why you think it should be accepted or rejected.

Investigation 6:

Adaptations to the Ocean

Key Question

Before you begin, first think about this key question.

How are fish and marine mammals adapted to live in the ocean?

Think about what you know about ocean water and the depth of the ocean. How are fish adapted to life in the ocean?

Share your thoughts with others in the class. Record the class discussion in your journal.

Materials Needed

For this investigation, your group will need:

- empty, plastic film storage container
- weights (metal washers)
- clear, tall container full of water (aquarium or pitcher)
- pushpin
- pencil
- Alka-Seltzer® tablet
- poster paper

Investigate

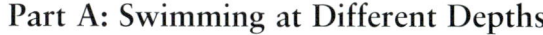

Part A: Swimming at Different Depths

1. In this investigation you will model how a marine fish or mammal is able to swim at different depths in the ocean.

Fill a film container with water and place it in a clear container of water (a clear pitcher or aquarium, for example). This is your "fish."

a) Is the film container more dense or less dense than the water? How can you tell?

2. In your group, discuss how you could make your fish sink.

   Design an experiment you could try to make the fish sink to the bottom of the container of water.

   a) Record your design in your journal.

3. After your teacher has approved your design, perform your experiment.

   a) Record your results in your journal. Make a chart like the one below, or design one of your own.

   b) Is the film container more dense or less dense than the water now? How can you tell?

Inquiry

Initial Experiments

Often, a scientific investigation begins with a series of simple, informal experiments, designed to test predictions about how to solve a problem. The outcome of these tests may not solve the problem, but the results may be useful in later investigations. Thus, good record-keeping is essential.

Trial #	Description	Result
1.		
2.		
Etc.		

4. Try to make your fish sink beneath the surface of the water, without letting it settle on the bottom.

   a) Record the details of your initial experiments on the chart in your journal.

   b) How easy is it to make the container "sink, without allowing it to sink all the way to the bottom?

5. Share the results of your experiment with other groups in your class.

   a) Which group had the best results? Describe their methods.

6. Many fish spend time at a number of different depths. Your fish must be able to live and reproduce in the water. To do so it will need to be able to raise and lower itself in the water. One way that fish are able to do this is by using gas to make them more or less buoyant. You will now attempt to model this.

   Using a pushpin, poke five holes in both the top and bottom of the container.

   Use the sharpened end of a pencil to widen the holes slightly. The holes must be between 1 to 2 mm in diameter.

7. Look back at your initial experiments in which you tried to get your model fish to sink without settling on the bottom.

   Add just enough mass to your fish to make it sink.

   Put the cap back on the film container and place it in on its side in the water.

   a) Describe what happens to your fish.

8. Place an Alka-Seltzer tablet in the container of water. (Your teacher may wish to demonstrate this.)

   Observe what happens to the tablet.

   a) Record your observations.

9. Add an Alka-Seltzer tablet to the film container and place the cap back on.

   a) Before you actually place the container in the water, predict what you think will happen. Record your prediction.

   b) Place the container on its side on the surface of the water. Record your observations. How accurate was your prediction? Did your fish manage to raise and lower itself in the water?

   c) How realistic do you think your model was in representing how a fish raises and lowers itself in the ocean?

Part B: Food Chains in the Ocean

1. A food chain shows a step-by-step sequence of who eats whom. At the bottom of the food chain is a plant, or some other organism, that gets its energy from a non-living source. The plants or other organisms are called producers because they can manufacture their own food. Without them, there would be no food, directly or indirectly, for the other organisms.

Example of a grazer food chain on land

a) As a group, name four organisms that form a marine food chain. Draw the food chain in your journal.

b) The food chain in the diagram uses arrows to show the direction of the flow of energy. Use arrows to describe the flow of energy in your food chain. (In other words, from where does each organism get the energy it needs to live.)

2. The characteristics of an organism that make it "better suited" to its environment are called adaptations.

a) Describe several adaptations that allow each organism to feed or obtain energy.

b) Describe several other adaptations that allow each organism to survive and reproduce.

3. Summarize your group's food chain and the adaptations of the organisms in the form of a poster. Include pictures and a summary of your group's discussion.

   Share your posters with other members of the class.

Part C: Marine Organisms and Their Environment

1. The oceans present a great range of environments for marine organisms. That is because the physical and chemical nature of the oceans varies quite a bit from place to place. The diagram shows the major environments in the world's oceans.

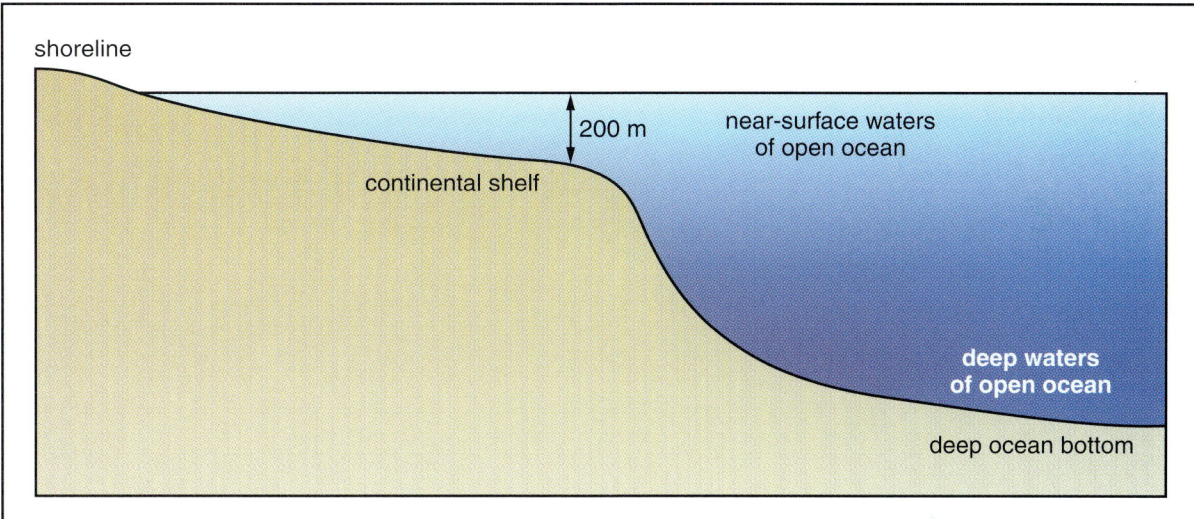

These environments can be described in terms of several characteristics. Here is a list of the most important ones:

- temperature
- pressure
- salinity
- currents
- dissolved oxygen
- nutrients
- light

a) In your group, discuss and record in your journal what each environment might be like.

2. On a large piece of poster board, draw a 5-by-7 grid of large boxes, seven horizontally and five vertically. Make the grid of boxes large enough to fill most of the poster board.

a) Label the grid as shown.

	temperature	pressure	salinity	currents	dissolved oxygen	nutrients	light
shoreline							
continental shelf							
near-surface waters of open ocean							
deep waters of open ocean							
deep ocean bottom							

b) Write in the upper parts of the boxes, in black, what you think the characteristics are like in each of the environments. Use a pencil, not a pen, because you are likely to want to make many changes as your thinking and discussions proceed! You might want to use words like "high," "low," "weak," or "strong." Use longer descriptions or comments if you think they are needed.

3. Here is a list of most of the major kinds of marine organisms:

- *phytoplankton* (small, free-floating, organisms that can make their own food)

- *zooplankton* (small, free-floating, organisms that cannot make their own food)

- *marine invertebrates* (mollusks, corals, etc.)

- *fish* (bass, tuna, mackerel, etc.)

- *large marine mammals* (whales, porpoises, etc.)

Microphotograph of a planktonic foraminifer

Grouper fish

Soft coral

Humpback whale

Think about how these kinds of organisms are adapted to the environments shown on your poster board.

a) With a red pencil, write the names of one or more of these kinds of organisms in one or more of the boxes on your poster board, below the dashed lines.

b) Beneath the names, with a black pencil, write a few words about how the organisms are adapted to the environmental conditions that are associated with the box.

4. In a class discussion, compare the results of all the small groups. Discuss the differences between the groups.

As You Read...
Think about:

1. *What are the environmental characteristics of the ocean that vary?*

2. *Which characteristic of the ocean remains fairly constant?*

3. *What are some ways that animals adapt to life in the ocean?*

4. *How are fish able to swim at different levels in the water?*

5. *What are the most important type of marine plants? Why does most life in the ocean depend on them?*

Digging Deeper

ADAPTING TO LIFE IN THE OCEAN
The Ocean Environment

The ocean environment is highly varied. Water temperature is as warm as 30°C in some areas of the ocean surface at low latitudes (in the tropical areas). The water temperature is not much above zero in the deep ocean. Even at the surface at high latitudes (the polar areas) the water temperature is frigid.

Water pressure increases with depth. It is over 1000 times atmospheric pressure in the deepest parts of the ocean.

In most of the deep ocean, currents are only a few centimeters per second, but in many shallow coastal areas the currents can be stronger than a meter per second.

The amount of salt in the water of the open oceans does not change very much. However, the salinity of the water is lower where major rivers flow into the ocean.

Light, which is essential for plant growth, is limited to the upper part of the oceans. Not much light reaches depths below about 100 m.

Oxygen dissolved in the water is essential for marine animals. Cold water can hold much more oxygen than warm water. Surface waters at high latitudes have relatively high concentrations of oxygen. This oxygen is carried to low latitudes by slow-flowing bottom currents. Oxygen is also abundant near the ocean surface, where it is obtained directly from the atmosphere. Oxygen is very low, however, in the mid-depths of the ocean.

Nutrients are important for plant growth. Nutrients are reduced in surface waters, where plants can grow because of sunlight. In some areas of the ocean upwelling brings deeper water that is rich in nutrients to the surface. Plant

growth is most abundant there. The best fishing in the oceans is in places where upwelling causes plant growth, which in turn feeds animals higher in the food chain.

Adaptations

Over geologic time, a length of time that is hard for us to imagine, plants and animals have changed in ways that make them "best suited" to live in a particular part of the ocean. Specific ways that organisms have developed to survive and reproduce in a particular kind of environment are called adaptations.

Coloration is a good example. Some organisms that float freely in surface waters are almost transparent, and are almost invisible. Many organisms that live on the bottom have developed colors that blend with their surroundings, as a kind of natural camouflage. Swim bladders allow fish to change depth without using much muscular energy. Fish have a streamlined shape that allows them to swim fast without much resistance from the surrounding water. Marine mammals, like whales, also have streamlined shapes. You can appreciate the importance of water resistance when you compare your beautiful knife-edge dive with a belly-flop! These are only a few of the great variety of adaptations that marine biologists have recognized.

Stonefish

Manta ray

Swimming of Fish

Many kinds of marine animals float passively in the water. Others move from place to place under their own power. The streamlined shape of fish, and their strong muscles that move tail and fins, make fish the best swimmers in the ocean. Most fish can live in a wide range of water depths. Small internal gas-filled pouches, called swim bladders, allow many kinds of fish to change their water depth without having to expend much energy.

Barracuda

A fish without a swim bladder is more dense than seawater, because fish bones are much more dense than seawater. Many fish that live on the bottom don't need swim bladders, because they never swim very far above the bottom. Fish that live in some range of depth above the bottom have solved the problem of buoyancy by developing swim bladders. They adjust the volume of gas in their swim bladders so that they have exactly the same density as the seawater at the given depth in the ocean. As they move upward, they add some gas to the bladder, to become slightly less dense. As they move downward, they absorb some gas from the bladder, to become slightly more dense. The gas in the swim bladder is exchanged with gas dissolved in the bloodstream of the fish.

The Food Chain

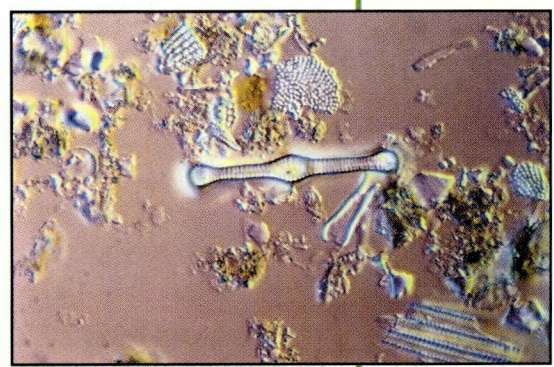

Benthic, or bottom-dwelling, diatom

All animals need a source of energy for their life activities. Almost all of this energy begins with plants. Plants use sunlight and nutrients to make their tissues, by a process called photosynthesis. The most important kinds of marine plants are tiny, free-floating plants called phytoplankton. Diatoms, shown in the photograph, are one of the most important kinds of phytoplankton.

If the right nutrients are available, phytoplankton grow in enormous numbers in the upper part of the oceans, where there is plenty of sunlight. Many marine animals eat the phytoplankton. Even whales, the largest animal in the oceans, feed on phytoplankton! Animals that feed only on plant material are called herbivores ("plant eaters"). Many other marine animals, called carnivores ("meat eaters") eat other animals. Typically, larger animals eat smaller animals. You've probably all seen cartoons of big fish eating little fish, and even bigger fish eating the big fish. For the most part, things really happen that way in the oceans. This is called the food chain. Because there are so many kinds of organisms in the ocean, there is actually an enormous number of different versions of the food chain. It's even better to think in terms of a "food web," with many interconnected pathways, rather than a simple chain.

Usually, only four or five different kinds of organisms, at different "eating levels," are involved in a food chain. You might wonder why there aren't more levels. The answer has to do with energy. Plants store energy by photosynthesis. The animals that eat the plants (and the animals that eat those animals) use that energy for themselves. Much of the energy is used only to maintain the organism in a state of health. That is, the animals need energy for breathing, digestion, and movement. For this reason, the energy available for the next level in the food chain becomes less. The result is that not much energy is left for marine animals (sharks are a good example) at the top of the food chain.

Review and Reflect

Review

1. How does a swim bladder enable a fish to regulate its position in the water?

2. What is an adaptation? Give some examples of adaptations of marine organisms.

3. What is a food chain? Give an example of a marine food chain.

Reflect

4. Describe at least three ways that being able to raise and lower itself in the water could help a fish survive and reproduce.

5. How did adding an Alka-Seltzer tablet to your model of a fish change the fish's density?

6. Explain how energy is lost at each step in a food chain.

Thinking about the Earth System

7. Explain how a marine organism can be adapted to elements in the hydrosphere, geosphere, and atmosphere.

Thinking about Scientific Inquiry

8. How did your initial experiments help you make a better prediction?

Investigation 7:

Investigating a Place in the Ocean

Putting It All Together

Key Question

Before you begin, first think about this key question.

How can you describe a place in the ocean?

Think about what you have learned so far about oceans. What kinds of things can you study in the ocean?

Share your thinking with others in your class. Keep a record of the discussion in your journal.

Materials Needed

For this investigation your group will need:

• access to reference materials on the ocean

• clear plastic container (like a deli sandwich box)

• any materials necessary to build a model of the sea floor

• transparency pens

• transparency sheets or a lid for the plastic container

Investigate

1. Choose an ocean place from the list below. Your group will research this place, investigating features of the water and the sea floor.

• *Great Barrier Reef*

• *Japan Trench*

• *Marianas Trench*

- *Hawaiian Islands*
- *Mid-Atlantic Ridge*
- *Belize Reef*
- *Peru Trench*
- *Bering Strait*

2. Obtain a fact sheet from your teacher with information that will help you begin your research.

You will need to supplement this with information obtained at your library, over the Internet, and from other sources.

You should investigate the following characteristics of your ocean location:

- physical features of the sea floor;
- geologic history;
- nearest land masses;
- plate tectonic setting;
- unique properties of seawater in this area;
- surface currents;
- types and characteristics of living things, the animals that live there and the kinds of plants that are part of the food chain;
- changes in seawater and life forms with depth;
- how the Earth systems interact, and
- any other relevant and important information.

a) Make notes in your journal as you conduct your research.

b) Write a report detailing your findings. Include labeled figures, maps, drawings and text. This should not be a long report; however, it must be in your own words and all sources used as reference materials must be listed. Divide the work equally.

Inquiry

Using References as Evidence

When you write a science report, the information you gather from books, magazines, and the Internet comes from scientific investigations. Just as in your experiments, the results can be used as evidence. Sometimes, enough new evidence accumulates that make ideas change drastically. In the late 1960s and early 1970s, enough new evidence for plate tectonics accumulated for it to be widely accepted by scientists. Until then, however, it was only a hypothesis—and one that inspired lots of arguments at that! Because evidence, like an idea, is important, you must always list the source of your evidence. This not only gives credit to the person who wrote the work, but it allows others to examine it and decide for themselves whether or not it makes sense.

3. Build a model of your ocean place.

    Using a clear plastic container, construct a model that
    shows the topography of the sea floor and nearby land
    masses. Although your teacher may provide some
    materials, you will probably want to supplement these
    with your own.

4. Cut a transparency sheet to match the top of your model
    or, if your container has a clear lid, you may use this to
    label your model.

    a) Draw latitude and longitude markings on the
       transparency. In addition mark the points of the
       compass (North, South, East and West), direction of
       surface currents, the scale, and any other important
       features.

5. Present your model to the class.

    Listen carefully to other students' presentations. You will
    be responsible for knowing important details of all groups'
    ocean places—not just your own.

    a) Record notes about the research of other groups in
       your journal.

Review and Reflect

Review

1. What causes an ocean trench?

2. What kinds of adaptations would an animal need to live deep in the ocean?

3. Which of the ocean places in this investigation occur along tectonic plate boundaries?

4. Where do most of the ocean's plants live?

Reflect

5. Which of the ocean places in this investigation would be a good place to catch fish? Explain your answer.

6. Of all the places studied in this investigation, which do you think is the most important? There is no right or wrong answer, of course, so be sure to give a detailed explanation of your opinion.

Thinking about the Earth System

7. Write any new connections you found in this investigation. Add them to your *Earth System Connection* sheet.

Thinking about Scientific Inquiry

8. Why is research an important part of inquiry?

9. Why is it necessary to list your sources when doing a research project?

Reflecting

Back to the Beginning

You have been investigating oceans in many ways. How have your ideas changed since the beginning of the investigation? Look at the following questions and write down your ideas in your journal.

- What is an ocean?
- What makes ocean water move?
- Why does the ocean floor look the way it does?
- How does the ocean affect living things?

How has your thinking about oceans changed?

Thinking about the Earth System

Consider what you have learned about the Earth system. Refer to the *Earth System Connection* sheet that you have been building up throughout this module.

- What connections between oceans and the Earth system have you been able to find?

Thinking about Scientific Inquiry

You have used inquiry processes throughout the module. Review the investigations you have done and the inquiry processes you have used.

- What scientific inquiry processes did you use?
- How did scientific inquiry processes help you learn about oceans?

Not so much an ending as a new beginning!

This investigation into oceans is now completed. However, this is not the end of the story. You will see the importance of oceans where you live, and everywhere you travel. Be alert for opportunities to observe the importance of oceans and add to your understanding.

The Big Picture

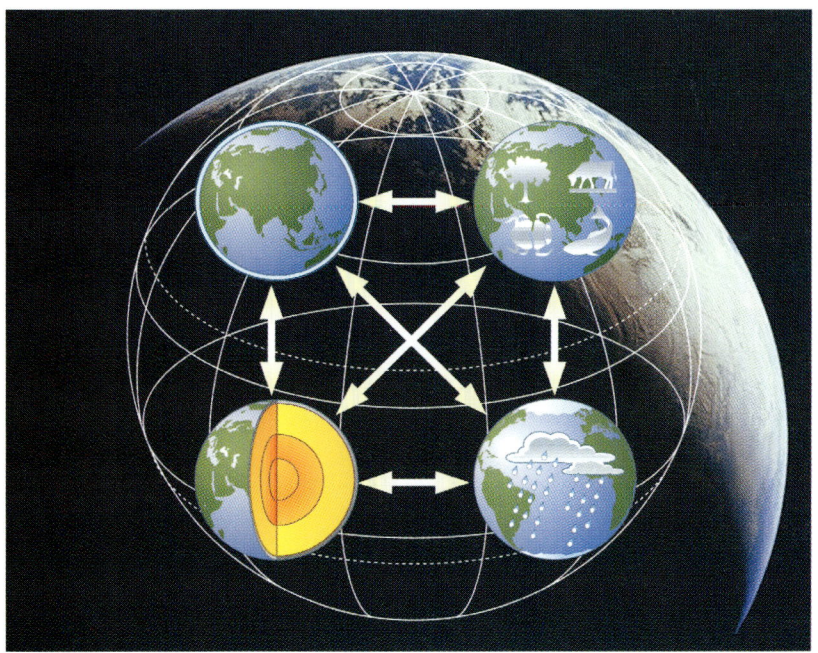

Key Concepts

Earth is a set of closely linked systems.

Earth's processes are powered by two sources: the Sun, and Earth's own inner heat.

The geology of Earth is dynamic, and has evolved over 4.5 billion years.

The geological evolution of Earth has left a record of its history that geoscientists interpret.

We depend upon Earth's resources—both mined and grown.

Glossary

Abyssal plain – A usually extensive sea-floor area with relatively little relief (change in elevation).

Adaptations – Specific ways that organisms have developed to survive and reproduce in a particular kind of environment.

Atmosphere – The layer of gases that surrounds the Earth. The atmosphere is a mixture of several gases.

Atom – A unit of matter composed of a nucleus and orbiting electrons; the smallest indivisible form of an element that maintains that element's chemical characteristics.

Bathymetric map – A topographical map of the bed of the ocean or any other body of water.

Biosphere – The part of the Earth System that includes all living organisms (animals and plants) and also dead and decaying plant matter.

Carnivore – An animal that eats other animals for its food.

Chemical composition – The make-up of a substance or material, in terms of the chemical elements.

Climate – Condition of the atmosphere over a long period at a place on Earth.

Concentrated – Said of a material which has a relatively high proportion of a particular substance.

Conductivity – The property of transmitting heat or electricity. Electrical conductivity is the ability of a substance to conduct an electrical current.

Continent – One of the Earth's major land masses.

Continental rise – The part of the continental margin built up of sediments between the continental slope and the abyssal plain.

Continental shelf – The gently sloping (0.1°) part of the continental margin between the shoreline and the continental slope. It is the part of the continent that is submerged below shallow seas.

Continental slope – The steeply sloping (3–6°) part of the continental margin between the continental shelf and the continental rise.

Control – A part of an experiment that is not altered. The control allows the experimenter to compare results to a standard.

Controlled test – An experiment. One in which all other variables are held constant except for one. This procedure allows the experimenter to find out which variable in the test is giving a particular result.

Crest (of a wave) – The highest part of a wave.

Cross section – A diagram showing features along a vertical plane.

Crust – The outermost layer of the Earth, composed of rock, sediment, and soil, representing less than 0.1% of the Earth's total volume.

Data – Observations, both quantitative and qualitative, that result from an experiment or a study.

Density – Mass per unit volume.

Dissolve – To put a solid into solution.

Earthquake – A sudden motion or trembling in the Earth caused by the abrupt release of slowly accumulated strain.

Earth System – A term used to describe the Earth as a set of closely interacting systems, including all sub-systems such the geosphere, lithosphere, atmosphere, hydrosphere, biosphere, and others.

Echo sounder – An instrument used to measure the depth of water using sonar.

Electron – Negatively charged particle that "orbits" the atomic nucleus.

Environment – Surroundings, including both living and non-living factors.

Equator – The line on the Earth's surface formed by the intersection with the plane passing through the center of the Earth and perpendicular to the axis of rotation. It is at 0° latitude.

Erosion – The weathering away of soil or rock by weathering, and the action of streams, glaciers, waves, wind, and underground water.

Estimate – A mathematical approximation.

Evaporation – The process of changing from a liquid to a gas.

Evaporites – Sediments that are deposited from a solution as a result of evaporation of the water.

Evidence – Data that support or refute a scientific conclusion.

Fair test – An experiment in which only one variable is tested at a time. A fair test also involves a control, a well-defined research question, collection and verification of data, and repeated trials.

Fault – A fracture or fracture zone along which there has been movement of the rock masses on either side relative to one another.

Fetch – The distance that the wind can blow over a body of water.

Flawed test – One in which the rules of fair testing have not been observed. A test could be flawed for a number of reasons: the test did not have a control, more than one variable was altered at a time, the research question didn't fit the test, the data were not collected or recorded accurately, or only one trial was done.

Food chain – A step-by-step sequence of who eats whom.

Geology – The study of planet Earth: the materials of which it is made, the processes that act on these materials, the products formed, and the history of the planet and all its life forms since its origin.

Geoscientist – A person who is trained in and works in any of the geological sciences.

Geosphere – The part of the Earth System that includes the crust, mantle, and core.

Gyre – A large clockwise and counterclockwise surface current in one of the major ocean basins.

Herbivore – An animal that feeds only on plant matter.

Hydrosphere – The part of the Earth System that includes all the planet's water, including oceans, lakes, rivers, ground water, ice, and water vapor.

Hypothesis – A statement that can be proved or disproved by experimental or observational evidence.

Inquiry – The process of finding answers to questions through a variety of methods. These can include research, fair testing, using models, asking experts, or many other methods.

Inquiry processes – The methods used by scientists to find answers to questions. They include hypothesizing, observing, recording, analyzing, concluding, communicating, and others.

Inquiry questions – Questions designed to be answered through a systematic, scientific process.

Ion – An atom that has an electric charge.

Kinetic energy – The energy of motion.

Latitude (lines of) – Angular distance of a point on the Earth's surface north or south of the Equator, measured in degrees with the Equator being at latitude 0°, the North Pole at latitude 90°N, and the South Pole at latitude 90°S.

Lithosphere – The outermost solid material of the Earth, which does not flow as part of mantle convection cells.

Lithospheric plates – Segments of the lithosphere which move relative to other segments.

Longitude (lines of) – Angular distance between the meridian of a given place and the prime meridian of Greenwich, England (which has longitude 0°), measured east or west to a maximum value of 180°.

Magma – Naturally occurring molten rock material, generated within the Earth from which igneous rocks are derived through solidification and related processes.

Mantle – The zone of the Earth beneath the crust and above the core. It is divided into the upper mantle and the lower mantle.

Marine organisms – Plants, animals, and other living things that dwell in (and are adapted to) the ocean.

Mid-oceanic ridge – A continuous median mountain ridge extending through an ocean, which is seismically active with a central rift valley and rugged topography. Mid-oceanic ridges are thought to be the source of new crustal material.

Model – A representation of a process, system, or object that is too big, too small, too unwieldy, or too unsafe to test directly.

Modeling – The process by which a representation of a process, system, or object is used to investigate a scientific question.

Observations – Data collected using the senses.

Oceanographer – A scientist trained and working in the field of oceanography.

Oceanography – The study of the ocean, including its boundaries and bottom topography, the physics and chemistry of seawater, the types of currents, and the many phases of marine biology.

Organisms – Living things.

Physical properties – The physical characteristics of materials or substances, such as melting point, density, color, etc., that can be used to identify the material or substance.

Plate – A rigid thin segment of the Earth's lithosphere; same as lithospheric plate.

Plate boundary – A zone of seismic and tectonic activity when two lithospheric (tectonic) plates are in contact with one another.

Plate tectonics – The theory in which the lithosphere is divided into a number of plates, and the study of how the plates move and interact with one another.

Potential energy – The energy associated with height.

Precipitation – The process of separating a mineral from a solution by evaporation.

Prediction – A reasonable estimate of the outcome of a scientific test. Predictions are based upon previous experiments and other research.

Properties – The characteristics of a material or substance.

Qualitative properties – Features that are described without using numbers, such as color, odor, and so on.

Quantitative properties – Features that are described by making measurements using numbers, such as mass (number of grams), length (number of meters), and so on.

Salinity – The concentration of salts in seawater.

Scale – A comparison of the measurement on a drawing to the actual measurement of the object.

Sonar – An acronym of "sound navigation and ranging," a method used in oceanography to study the ocean floor.

Sounding – The measurement of water depth taken from a ship.

Stone – A general term for the rock that is used in construction.

Subduction zone – A long belt on the Earth where one plate dives down beneath another plate at some angle.

Tectonic plate – Another term for a lithospheric plate.

Theory – A hypothesis that has never been disproved.

Thermocline – The depth zone where the temperature of a body of water changes from warm to cold.

Topographic map – A map showing the natural and man-made configuration of a land surface, other features of the land surface, commonly by use of contour lines, colors, and symbols.

Topography – The configuration of a land surface, including its relief and the position of its natural and human-made features.

Transparent – A material that easily allows light to pass through.

Trough (of a wave) – The lowest part of a wave.

Variables – The things about an experiment that can be changed by the researcher. In a fair test, only one variable is changed at a time.

Verify – Confirm. In science, this means that someone checks your procedures and findings.

Volcano – A vent in the surface of the Earth through which magma and associated gases and ash erupt.

Wave – A motion that travels through a material and carries energy from one place to another; an undulating movement in a body of water shown by an alternating rise and fall of the water surface.

Wave action – The process by which land is eroded and sediment is moved by water waves.

Wave height – The vertical distance between the trough and crest of a wave.

Wavelength – The distance between successive wave crests (or any other equivalent points) in a series of waves.

Wave period – The time it takes two crests to pass the same point.

Weathering – The complex of natural processes, both physical and chemical, that act to change exposed rock into mineral and rock particles and chemical compounds in solution.

The American Geological Institute and Investigating Earth Systems

Imagine more than 500,000 Earth scientists worldwide sharing a common voice, and you've just imagined the mission of the American Geological Institute. Our mission is to raise public awareness of the Earth sciences and the role that they play in mankind's use of natural resources, mitigation of natural hazards, and stewardship of the environment. For more than 50 years, AGI has served the scientists and teachers of its Member Societies and hundreds of associated colleges, universities, and corporations by producing Earth science educational materials, *Geotimes*–a geoscience news magazine, GeoRef–a reference database, and government affairs and public awareness programs.

So many important decisions made every day that affect our lives depend upon an understanding of how our Earth works. That's why AGI created *Investigating Earth Systems*. In your *Investigating Earth Systems* classroom, you'll discover the wonder and importance of Earth science. As you investigate minerals, soil, or oceans — do field work in nearby beaches, parks, or streams, explore how fossils form, understand where your energy resources come from, or find out how to forecast weather — you'll gain a better understanding of Earth science and its importance in your life.

We would like to thank the National Science Foundation and the AGI Foundation Members that have been supportive in bringing Earth science to students. The Chevron Corporation provided the initial leadership grant, with additional contributions from the following AGI Foundation Members: Anadarko Petroleum Corp., Baker Hughes Foundation, Barrett Resources Corp., BPAmoco Foundation, Burlington Resources Foundation, Conoco Inc., Consolidated Natural Gas Foundation, Diamond Offshore Co., EEX Corp., ExxonMobil Foundation, Global Marine Drilling Co., Halliburton Foundation, Inc., Kerr McGee Foundation, Maxus Energy Corp., Noble Drilling Corp., Occidental Petroleum Charitable Foundation, Parker Drilling Co., Phillips Petroleum Co., Santa Fe Snyder Corp., Schlumberger Foundation, Shell Oil Company Foundation, Southwestern Energy Co., Texaco, Inc., Texas Crude Energy, Inc., Unocal Corp. USX Foundation (Marathon Oil Co.).

We at AGI wish you success in your exploration of the Earth System!

Michael J. Smith
Director of Education, AGI

Marcus E. Milling
Executive Director, AGI